They All
Slumbered
and
Slept

They All Slumbered and Slept

The Year 2000—What Happened?

Marvin Byers

Hebron Press
Section 0374
P. O. Box 02-5289
Miami, FL   33102-5289

Cover design by Carlos Macías

ISBN 1-59352-022-0

For Worldwide Distribution
Printed in the U.S.A.

1-800-LAST DAY
minheb@c.net.gt

Call us to obtain copies of this, and other books by the same author, in English or Spanish, or see the addresses listed in the end of the book.

Contents

Dear Reader,

Due to a glitch in the computer program that was used to format the page layout of this book, there are a number of hyphenation errors in this first printing. I trust that this will not hinder you from receiving a blessing from the message presented here.

Yours in Christ,

Marvin Byers

A Personal Note

Dear Friend,

Please forgive me.

For 30 years, between 1970 and the year 2000, I believed and taught with all my heart that the Lord would return in the year 2000. Because of the infamous Y2K, by 1998, many, if not most Christians came to believe that either the Lord would return in 2000 or else that year would somehow be related to the beginning of the end. When the Lord did not return, many hearts were negatively impacted, causing them to react in various ways. Some mocked, some lost all desire to understand the last days, others were confused and their faith was even shaken, while others made excuses. Yet, a few recognized that, as I Corinthians 13:12 tells us, we see through a glass darkly. Instead of "throwing in the towel" on the study of God's prophetic message, these believers still continue to seek for understanding on this subject.

I want to fulfill a promise that I made long before the year 2000. I said, "If the Lord does not return in 2000 I will ask the Body of Christ to forgive me, and I will do so in writing." I would like to fulfill that promise here and ask for forgiveness from all those who were affected negatively by my teaching regarding the return of the Lord. My prayer has been, and continues to be, that even if their confidence in me has been destroyed, nothing will be able to shake their faith in the Lord and their love for His Word.

With sincere love and joy, I dedicate this book's message to the people who have not only revealed a loving heart toward me, as a person, but also toward the areas of truth that the Lord has permitted us to see and teach together. Because of these people, I ask for forgiveness here for any and all of my errors or lack of clear understanding regarding the last days. Instead of mocking or criticizing, many have asked me, with sincere and humble hearts, if the Lord has given me any insight into what went wrong.

Such questions moved me to write this book.

Although we still see through a glass darkly, I believe we see more clearly today than we did even four years ago. There are many who love the truth. There are also many who continue to love the approximately one-third of the Bible that deals with the last days. I realize that some might consider what I share in this book to be an excuse. However, my hope is that some of those who continue searching the Scriptures for answers will find in this book at least a partial answer to what happened, or did not happen, in the year 2000.

It is my sincere desire that the Lord will cause this book to bring water for thirsty souls and food for hungry hearts; that He will give to each of us His great mercy and the grace required to seek Him more than ever, as we watch and wait for His appearing.

Marvin Byers
April 24, 2003

1998—Looking Back

In 1998, the third edition of my book, *The Final Victory: The Year 2000?*, was published. Especially for those who read that book, I want to share an important link to this book by recalling what was written nearly two years before the year 2000. My hope is that each of us will receive God's grace today to experience what was written then. Please note that back then it was apparent that, biblically, a delay might be involved in the events of the last days. I offer this as a point of reference, before we enter into the theme of this present book. Even though much more was said about a delay in that book, here are the very last paragraphs:

"... He invites us to embrace the cross. He invites us to offer to Him our bodies as a living sacrifice that the world may see the life of the crucified Savior in us and be drawn to Him (Jn. 12:32; Gal. 3:1).

"The world will see Jesus only as the Church learns to spend time with Him, beholding the beauty of the Lord, as David desired to do daily (Ps. 27:4). From that secret place we will shout the message to the world with our lives and with our words. We will win their hearts, and evangelize this globe before He returns. We don't need more sermons or better sermons. We don't need to learn how to convince people to follow us through our own wisdom and words. We need more of His presence, which will break the hardest heart, convince the wisest skeptic, convict the most pious sinner of his need, and comfort the comfortless. Those who are bathed in His presence will do all these things without needing to resort to the strength and efforts of the flesh. They will manifest the strength and authority of the Lion, but they will do so with the mind and nature of the Lamb. They will win the war, and be

part of the final victory in the year 2000. And if His coming is delayed or our understanding is in error, they will continue to be thankful for every additional day that they, as well as others, are being granted to know the King in still deeper ways. Will you be one of those whom the Lord chooses to visit in a new and deeper way in these last days? He is willing if you are. He longs to visit those whose desire is toward Him. May we be willing to lay aside the pursuit of this world and its pleasures to seek the Lord and His favor as never before." (Page 347)

That was my heart's desire for each of us back in 1998, and that is my heart's desire now—more than ever. I realize that by writing this book some will, without regard to what I said then, be even more critical toward me now, concluding that I am simply attempting to make excuses. Those whose hearts mock and become critical can almost never be persuaded.

My goal is not to try to convince anyone of anything, but I do have a deep concern for the humble hearts who still seek for a greater understanding of truth. Because we continue to see the last days through a glass darkly, some have decided that they are no longer interested in seeing at all. But there are still some who long to see more clearly and want to know where I, along with others, have made mistakes or misunderstood the very small revelation that the Lord has allowed us to receive.

One reason the Lord allows us to see only part of the truth in any area is to keep us humble before Him. If we were to receive a complete revelation of truth, we would have no need of others and undoubtedly would become puffed up with pride. Of course, we are humbled even more when we realize that we have taught an incomplete or even incorrect understanding of God's Word. In such cases, we need to sincerely repent before God and man.

Besides using our mistakes to humble us, God also uses them to reveal what is in the hearts of others. Very often, the doctrinal mistakes of a leader become the perfect pretext for mutiny in the heart of anyone who is motivated by carnal ambition. In such a person's heart, doctrinal error is justification for them to rise up, divide the church, and start their own work; or, they may simply attempt to stay in the church and cause dissension, which is usually worse. All this is frequently done under the guise of "a deep love for truth and the well-being of the sheep." The real issue is self-love and ambition.

If division and separation are justifiable any time there are doctrinal differences, then every person on earth would have to walk alone, since no two people are ever in total agreement regarding doctrine. If doctrinal purity regarding the last days is our basis for fellowship, then we will have precious little fellowship with others. Today, few groups in the Body of Christ are in harmony with one another regarding the Bible's prophetic message. There is only one correct understanding of God's prophetic message, and that one correct understanding is that which God Himself has. Certainly great differences of opinion and interpretation exist within the Church today on this subject. This proves one thing—that most or all of us continue to believe and teach at least some prophetic heresy. We should ask ourselves, "Is my brother's heresy any more dangerous than my own?"

Maybe we would never use incomplete or even incorrect doctrine as a pretext to divide a church, but we might react in other ways that reveal an unhealthy spiritual heart condition. For example, how do we react when we hear someone teaching something that differs with our doctrinal position? Do we mock that person in our heart, and sometimes with our words, because of his error or do we, instead, rejoice in the aspect of his message that is true? Paul tells us that love rejoices in the truth (I Cor. 13:6b). Love does not take pleasure in criticizing another's errors. Our reaction in the face of error often reveals whether our heart tends to show love or scorn. It also reveals if we are one of those who tend to doubt or tend to believe in our hearts. A mocking heart is almost always an unbelieving heart. Let me say here: I do not rejoice over those who may have erred by mocking me or anyone else. I desire for the Lord to grant them mercy and repentance, as we all need in every area of our lives.

Will you join me in seeking Him as never before? Let's ask the Lord to draw us into His presence. We need a heart that wants to sit at His feet and learn of Him Who is "meek and lowly," and Who has given to us His Spirit Who desires to teach us all things, even the secrets of the Lord that He desires to share with His close friends.

Chapter 1

Wrong? Or Incomplete Picture?

My wife, Barbara, and I became Israeli citizens in 1994. We "made aliyah." When a Jewish person leaves the nation in which he has lived and returns to the Promised Land, the Jewish people call this "making aliyah." This phrase conveys the idea of "going up" ("aliyah") to Zion. Upon arriving in Israel, we felt the Lord wanted us to simply live out the Christian life among the Jewish people living in the neighborhood where we rented a house in greater Jerusalem. We knew that most of our Jewish neighbors did not need to *hear* another message about their Messiah as much as they needed to *see* the message being lived before them.

In Israel there is a very powerful and well-funded religious intelligence organization. When they discover that a Jewish person believes in Yeshua (Jesus), they notify all the neighbors that a traitor is in their midst. From that day on, few if any of the neighbors will even say hello to such a person. We realized that if this happened, we would have very little opportunity to show them Jesus in any way whatsoever, and much less of a chance to talk with them about Him. We were living by the words of Augustine, who once told his disciples, "You are called to go out into the world and preach the gospel to every creature. Use words if necessary." We tend to use words first, when often the best way to preach the gospel is to use our life as a light in the midst of the darkness, without saying, a word until those around are dying to find out "what makes us tick."

The man we rented our house from lived directly behind us. He was a bank manager who observed at least the basic aspects of Judaism. Instead of trying to teach him about the Lord, I asked him one day to be my teacher and instruct me concerning Jewish orthodoxy. I did not tell him that my parents were both born-again believers. I simply explained that "I have never had much exposure to orthodox Judaism," a common situation for many people of Jewish descent.

He was delighted at the confidence I placed in him and was happy to instruct me. I explained to him that we had just moved to Israel and that we were not sure what type of work we would ultimately be engaged in there. I told him that I was involved in business, which, at that time was totally true. He was content with that explanation of our lives. I did not tell him that I was also a pastor, involved in the Lord's business as well.

As we became better friends, we tried to show him the love of Jesus in every way we could. He knew there was something different about us, but he didn't know what it was. He tried every way he could think of to find out who we were and what we were about. On a number of occasions, while I was writing, studying or praying in my office in the basement of our house, he knocked at the front door. Upon answering his knock, Barbara would tell him that she would go downstairs and call me. He would insist, "No, don't bother. I will go down myself." He wanted to discover what I was doing all day!

Of course, my office was filled with Bibles and Christian literature. Barbara and I both knew that if he ever set one foot into my office, our friendship would be over; he would feel very betrayed. So she would loudly insist that she would be the one to let me know he had arrived. She would make sure I could hear the commotion so I could come running out of my office and meet him on the stairs, explaining that my office was too messy for him to see at that moment (something that was *always* true). In fact, various translations of the Bible were almost always scattered around my room!

We had no idea to what degree his heart had responded to the love of Jesus until one evening, when the main sewer of our house became plugged. We were getting ready to leave on a late-night flight. Since our house was new, he first attempted to find the man who had installed the plumbing in the house. When that proved impossible, and since we needed to use the showers before our departure, he decided to do what he could to remedy the problem himself.

I could not believe what I saw, but even more amazing was what I heard from his mouth. This very respectable bank manager went outside, got down on his knees, opened up the cover on the main sewage line, and began to reach into the pipes and pull out everything that he could reach—with his bare hands! I stood there in awe and watched him. I had actually worked as a plumber for a short time many years before, but I could never have brought myself to do what he was doing. After removing quite a bit from the pipes, he stopped, looked up at me and said: "Marvin, I would never do this for any other man on earth." My heart broke. My spirit was humbled. Jesus had not needed my words or wisdom to convince this man of His love. He had simply lived His life out through us.

Some time after this, we knew it was time to let our landlord know what I was doing in my office—writing books. I explained to him that one book I had written was based on prophecies from Daniel, a Jewish prophet, and that I had shown why the Messiah would come in the year 2000. Of course, I realized that he might become very skeptical upon discovering this. To my surprise, that did not happen.

Rather, the very next day he asked his rabbi to come to his house. He told the rabbi that his unusual neighbor believed that the Messiah would come in the year 2000, and asked him if he had ever heard such a thing and if he thought it could be possible. Both to his surprise and mine (when he recounted this to me later), the rabbi told him that he had not only heard about that possibility but that many Jewish rabbis believed precisely the same thing; some were openly declaring it. Of course, he was delighted and even more open to us. When the day finally came when we shared openly with him about Jesus, it was obvious by the light that shone on his face that he understood that Jesus had died to be his Redeemer.

About two years later, for the very first time in my life, I had the opportunity to speak with an ultra-orthodox Jewish man. The ultra-orthodox are loath to speak to anyone who does not whole-heartedly follow orthodoxy, even if the person is a fellow Jew. My encounter with this man took place in a bookstore in the old city of Jerusalem. He was willing to speak to me only because I was trying to buy a reference book about Judaism for a friend. He probably assumed that since I was buying a book on Judaism, I would soon be a convert to orthodoxy and that he should help me. The salesman in the bookstore was trying to find the phone number of a store that might have had the book I wanted, when the ultra-orthodox man entered the store. The salesman asked him if he knew where I might find the book, so we began to talk.

It was the latter part of 1998, so I was still convinced that the year 2000 would be a very important year. Therefore, I asked him straight out, "What do you feel will happen in Israel in the immediate future?" Without the slightest delay, he responded, "There will be war very shortly and the Messiah will come in the year 2000." Of course, my next question was, "Why do you believe the Messiah will come in the year 2000?" To my surprise and delight, he opened his heart to me and began to share the history of his belief regarding this and why many rabbis believed the same.

Among the various biblical reasons for their belief, he shared with me a Jewish thought that I had been aware of for some years. He explained:

> For at least two to three thousand years, and possibly beginning with Moses, many rabbis have believed that the six days of labor and one day of rest that the Lord gave to man is a prophetic principle. Since a day with God is a thousand years, there will be six thousand years between Adam and the coming of the Messiah during which man will do his own works. After those days, God's people will have a day of rest that will last one thousand years.

> The rabbis know that there is an error of 230 years in the Jewish calendar. Therefore, the year 5770 on the Jewish calendar corresponds to the year 2000 on the Gregorian calendar and marks the end of 6,000 years of biblical history. The second most respected rabbi of Jewish history wrote over 400 years ago that if the Messiah did not come in the year 5770 that his disciples should burn all the books he had written.

After hearing this, I felt much better about having written a book predicting the coming of the Messiah in the year 2000. I felt that even if what I had written was mistaken, at least I had plenty of company—the spiritual leaders of God's chosen people, the Jews, who believed this for thousands of years before I came along. In fact, in his epistle, the Apostle Barnabas also mentioned the concept of six days symbolizing 6,000 years. The epistle Barnabas wrote is known to be genuine, used by different sectors of the early Church. So, the concept of the Messiah returning after 6,000 years is at least 2,000 years old!

Lest we forget the place that Israel continues to occupy in God's plan, Paul explains to us that God did not cast away nor reject Israel (Rom. 11:1-5). God will continue to deal with the Jewish people until they return to Him and are saved (Rom. 11:11-15, 25-26). We should also note Paul's declaration that *"blindness in part is happened to*

Israel" (Rom. 11:25b). If they are only partly blind, then they also partly see.

Although most Jewish people still cannot see Jesus as their Messiah, the truths from the Bible they *have* seen during the last 2,000 years are often real gems, as evidenced by rabbinical writings. We should therefore consider the possibility that they have had at least some biblical and logical basis for believing that the Messiah would establish His Kingdom on the earth around the year 2000.

I recently asked a pastor who fervently preached for years that the Lord would come in the year 2000, what he now feels about his message since the year 2000 has passed. He responded, "It was just my own concoction." Maybe that was true in his case, but we should ask, Was this also true for all the Christian and Jewish leaders who believed that the year 2000 would be significant? Was it all meaningless? Was it nothing more than millennial fever or a fleshly concoction by them all, including Barnabas? Or, could it be that we have overlooked some details in Scripture that shed further light on the timing of the Lord's coming? I have no interest in making the grave mistake of coming to the end of my life making excuses for my errors and incorrect teaching. But, on the other hand, there might be a different mistake that is almost as bad, and any of us could make it. John the Baptist made this mistake.

Few people today would even begin to consider themselves on the same spiritual level that John the Baptist attained. The Lord declared that he was the greatest prophet of all time. I would not begin to compare myself with John, but even this great prophet had both positive and negative lessons to teach us. One negative lesson we learn from John comes at the end of his life when he sent messengers to Jesus asking if He was really the Christ. John was asking whether or not he had made a mistake. Should he look for someone else instead of Jesus of Nazareth? He was doubting his own message! Of course, this also reveals the humility in John's heart. He was willing to reexamine his doctrinal positions rather than dogmatically continue in error all the way to his death.

Even so, is it not somewhat sad that the last thing we hear from John is an expression of doubt concerning the veracity of the very message he had spoken to Israel? The message in which he declared that Jesus was the Messiah? Of course, we find his Old Testament counterpart, Elijah, also ending his ministry with doubts, as well as complaints. Therefore, since John the Baptist was sent to Israel in the spirit and power of Elijah, it should not seem strange that he also ended his life battling unbelief and discouragement just as Elijah did.

Many Jewish people and Christians who believed that the Messiah would come in the year 2000 have also had battles with unbelief and discouragement. Although my wife and I did not have a battle in these areas, we *did* have a great battle. During many years, we presented what we and many others considered a strong biblical and historical basis for believing that the Lord would come in the year 2000. I doubt that even our closest friends were aware of the deep, heart-felt sorrow that we felt when it became apparent that the Lord was not going to come in the year 2000.

We were not saddened by the fact that we would personally be humiliated and face rejection. We all need to be humbled, and regardless of how that happens we should be willing to accept it as something that will be eternally good for us. Rather, we felt deep sorrow when we considered the many believers throughout the world who had been completely convinced of the importance of the year 2000, either through our teaching and that of many others. We had many questions: What would happen in their hearts? Would their faith be shaken? Would they doubt the truth of God's Word? Would they begin to follow after the world instead of the Lord? We are thankful that most of those we know have continued on with the Lord, but certainly doubts still exist in some, and they need to be conquered, because the biblical and historical evidence concerning the year 2000 really was convincing to them.

The evidence continues to be convincing. In 2002, a pastor who was totally unrelated to our ministry read the book I wrote, *The Final Victory: The Year 2000?*. Without any influence from me, that pastor came to the conclusion there was a great deal of weighty evidence presented there that pointed us to the year 2000 for the Lord's second coming. He later told me that he was glad he had not read my book before the year 2000 because the evidence was so convincing that he, too, would have expected the Lord to come at that time.

But the Lord did not come.

Something was clearly wrong and/or lacking in our message, or else in our understanding of the message. Will we also possibly end our lives in discouragement because of this, as John the Baptist and Elijah ended theirs?

I have stood before the people I pastor and told them that if the Lord shows me that all of that weighty evidence is false and without any relevance to the Lord's biblical calendar, I will admit this to them immediately. However, until then, maybe our mistake was that we saw through a glass darkly, and that we did not fully understand the message (or else that we failed to receive a vital part of the message). Of course, some will rightfully point out that, either way, what I shared was incorrect because the Lord did not return in the year 2000. This is one of the primary reasons for writing this book—to acknowledge this fact and ask forgiveness from the Body of Christ.

Another reason for writing this book is to consider some biblical facts that we (or at least I) did not understand before the year 2000. These facts will explain why I am not so quick to declare that what I saw, what many other Christians saw, and what the Jews have seen and believed for thousands of years, should be simply dismissed as nothing more than the concoctions of men.

The Lord did not return in the year 2000, so what should I do as a minister? For me, the easiest way out would be to stand up and tell the people whom I pastor that I was simply deceived. Some have counseled me to do so. Though I have not done this, most of the people that I have pastored for so many years have proven their genuine love for me. They have not rejected everything else I have taught them, nor have they rejected my ministry or me as a person. Obviously, a simple declaration stating that what I had shared with them about the Lord's calendar was completely wrong would have been easier for all of us. We could have put this whole thing behind us and moved on.

Furthermore, an outright admission of guilt would have freed us all from any further reproach and mocking. The whole issue would have died. By now, almost three years later, there would be no more reproach coming our way, as occasionally still happens. At least reproach would not still be coming from true Christians who know how to forgive and forget. Some might conclude that my problem is that I simply can't bring myself to admit that I was wrong. However, on various occasions, I have been willing to stand before people I have taught and admit my doctrinal mistakes. In light of eternity and the day of judgment, this is the wisest thing to do. As ministers, we will all have to give an account to the Lord for what we have taught. I would far rather straighten out my errors in this life in the presence of a few thousand people than wait to have them straightened out in the presence of the whole universe at the judgment seat.

No, my problem is not that I fear losing my reputation or the respect of others. With many, I have already lost both anyway. Rather, my problem is two-fold.

First, although I do not hope to end my life on a better plane than the one reached by John the Baptist, I *do* want to learn from his "mistake." The stories of both John and Elijah teach us that the best way to finish this life is by trusting the Lord in the midst of doubts and apparent contradictions to our teaching, especially if it turns out that our teaching actually came from the Lord. They both failed to do this near the end of their lives, though it is unlikely that either actually ended in this spiritual state.

Second, it's easy to pass through life saying, "Oops! I goofed!" It's easy to cancel all our mistakes with a simple apology. But it takes courage to find out *why* we goofed. Is there a lesson to be learned through our mistake? For example, was our mistake a result of total ignorance or even deception, or was our mistake a result of having information only partly correct or maybe even totally correct but woefully incomplete? I believe the latter is the issue. Our understanding was woefully incomplete, and in the following pages I want to share why.

On February 1, 2003, the space shuttle *Columbia* disintegrated over Palestine, Texas. It was later learned that some shuttle technicians on Earth had noticed that a piece of foam insulation had struck the left wing shortly after launch. Ceramic tiles are located in that area to protect the wing from overheating during the shuttle's reentry into Earth's atmosphere. Some technicians acknowledged a few days before the terrible accident that if some of the tiles on that wing had been knocked off during the launch, a disaster was in the making. Sometimes a very small error can produce enormously tragic results in any area, especially regarding the issue of God's truth and man's error.

Two other things were acknowledged by Ron Dittemore, the Director of Shuttle Operations. He said that powerful telescopes or satellites could have detected if damage had actually occurred to the tiles during launch. He said it would have been possible to send another shuttle into space to rescue the crew if they believed the shuttle *Columbia* might not have been able to land safely. Sometimes not having a complete picture can cause enormously tragic results. The Earth-based shuttle crew did not have a complete picture before the shuttle's return to Earth. Likewise, it is now apparent that many of us had an incomplete picture before the year 2000 regarding the timing of the Lord's return. The result has been great sorrow in the hearts of many, but this is not the time to jettison the search for truth any more than it is time to jettison mankind's continued space exploration.

In every area of our spiritual lives, we need to keep what came from the Lord and reject what did not. This book is not an attempt to make excuses for my mistake. I recognize that Jesus did not return in the year 2000; from any angle, I made a mistake. However, if we choose to sit in the seat of the scornful or yield to discouragement, we might end up throwing out wonderful truths in our haste to distance ourselves from what we perceive to be grave error. This would be especially tragic if that grave error later proved to be merely an incomplete understanding of certain details—similar to the missing tiles on the space shuttle!

Chapter 2

Seeking to Understand the Times Is Not Heretical

After what some call "the year 2000 debacle," many Christians have decided it is, at best, futile (maybe even heretical) to attempt to understand the timing of the Lord's return. It can only be heretical if following the example of the biblical prophets is heretical. James 5:10 tells us that the prophets are an example for us today. Their love of the truth and desire to understand God's plan should also be burning in our own hearts. Today, many have embraced great caution with regard to seeking understanding about last days, especially if the time of the Lord's return is involved. This concept would have seemed foreign to the prophets according to I Peter 1:10-11 (NIV):

> *Concerning this salvation, the prophets, who spoke of the grace that was to come to you, searched intently and with the greatest care, trying to find out the time and circumstances to which the Spirit of Christ in them was pointing when he predicted the sufferings of Christ and the glories that would follow.*

Mistakes and misunderstandings would not deter these prophets to give up their search. They were searching intently, with the greatest care, to find out the time of Christ's first coming, when He would come to suffer. Because the prophets were men, they too saw through a glass darkly, but obviously their mistakes did not cause them to give up the search. In the face of uncertainty and confusion, they must have redoubled their efforts time and again, using even greater care in their search for truth.

Before the year 2000, many sought to discover the time of Christ's second coming. Now, any mention of the timing of His coming is frowned upon. More than ever, there are naysayers who attempt to convince us that the Lord has hidden that timing and that we should not even attempt to discover His secret.

It is always humiliating to make a mistake. Certainly, many ministers have been badly burned in recent years by mistakes in their prophetic predictions. I know of some who, as a result, have declared that they will never again deal with the prophetic message. They feel safe now because they have spiritual fire insurance.

Could it be that their reaction is really just a manifestation of pride? They do not want to risk being humiliated again in their search for truth, so they have decided to stick to things so basic that they won't ever be guilty of being wrong again. If one of the costs of seeking and finding the truth is to risk the humiliation of being wrong, so be it! Who are we trying to impress anyway?

Just how important was it for Israel to understand the time of the Lord's first coming? Jesus gives us the answer in Luke 19:42-44, when He speaks to His people:

> ... *If thou hadst known, even thou, at least in this thy day, the things which belong unto thy peace! but now they are hid from thine eyes. For the days shall come upon thee, that thine enemies shall cast a trench about thee, and compass thee round, and keep thee in on every side, and shall lay thee even with the ground, and thy children within thee; and they shall not leave in thee one stone upon another; because thou knewest not the time of thy visitation.*

What a statement and what a warning! All these terrible judgments came on Israel because they did not know the *time* of their visitation. Specifically, they did not know when their Messiah was supposed to come. No wonder the prophets that ministered before Christ's first coming sought revelation regarding the time of His coming. They must have foreseen the danger involved in *not* knowing when He would come, and the damage ignorance of this truth would one day cause God's people. Those prophets are part of the "cloud of witnesses" mentioned in Hebrews 12:1. What would they answer today if we could ask them, "Is it heretical to search for understanding of the times?" Surely, their response would be with a shout loud enough to awaken us from our sleep. They would declare, "It is heretical *not* to search for understanding of the times, because failing to understand can bring great sorrow!"

When Christ came the first time, those who knew for certain that they were living in the days of His coming were actually looking for Him. They "found Him" as Philip declared Andrew, Peter and he had done in John 1:45. Usually, when we say we "found" someone, the implication is that we were looking for that person. For the Jews who knew the time of the Messiah's coming was at hand, it would not have been very difficult to discern who He was. After all, who else in Israel was raising the dead, giving sight to the blind, cleansing the lepers, healing the sick, and preaching the gospel of the Kingdom with an irresistible anointing from heaven? Jesus Himself answers this question in John 15:24 (NKJV):

> *If I had not done among them the works which no one else did, they would have no sin; but now they have seen and also hated both Me and My Father.*

No wonder the Lord rebuked the spiritual leaders of Israel for not discerning the times, specifically the time of His coming. He rebuked the Pharisees and Sadducees in Matthew 16:2b-3:

> *When it is evening, ye say, It will be fair weather: for the sky is red. And in the morning, It will be foul weather to day: for the sky is red and lowring. O ye hypocrites, ye can discern the face of the sky; but can ye not discern the signs of the times?*

Jesus said they were hypocrites with regard to discerning the times! In other words, they were only pretending that they couldn't discern the times. Knowing the time of the Messiah's coming would have forced them to look for and acknowledge His arrival once that time had come. It would not have been difficult for them to identify Him if they had been expecting Him. The glory of God that was revealed throughout Israel by the Only Begotten of the Father made it quite easy to discern the Messiah. The multitudes who proclaimed Him King during the triumphal entry recognized Him, yet the leaders pretended that they could not. They also pretended that they could not discern if it was even the time for the Messiah to come. An admission that it was the right time for His coming, and a recognition of the messianic credentials of Jesus of Nazareth, would have required them to forfeit their places of leadership in Israel, surrendering all to Him. This they were not willing to do.

Is there any position we fill, or any earthly thing we hold onto that might cause us to actually *hope* it is not time for the Lord to come? May our love for Him enable us to place all that we are and all that we possess on the Lord's altar of sacrifice. Paul tells us there is a crown of righteousness laid up for all those who love His appearing (II Tim. 4:8). Let's offer this simple prayer: "Lord, cause me to love your appearing so much that all the things of this world will grow strangely dim in the light of Your soon coming!"

Israel's leaders chose to ignore the time of His coming, probably pretending that no one could possibly know the time. This way they could continue in their own fleshly ways and cling to their positions. By pretending not to know, it was easy for them to put on a spiritual air and look wistfully toward the horizon, talking about how much they looked for and longed for the coming of their Messiah. All the while, their gaze was carefully lifted so that it passed over the head of the poor carpenter from Nazareth who stood before them, revealing the grace and glory of heaven. Maybe they even said to their followers, "Don't listen to anyone who talks about knowing the times. They are heretics who are only attempting to deceive you."

Isn't the same thing happening today? Is it wise to discount all the biblical and historical evidence that caused so many Jewish rabbis and Christian leaders to think that the Lord's coming was at hand in the year 2000? Rather than flippantly ignoring the evidence for that year, as well as the men who presented that evidence, it would seem wiser to humbly continue searching intently with the greatest care to understand the time. Maybe it was the Lord and not men who was giving understanding to His people before the year 2000, but we did not receive the whole message. In the following chapters, we will look at some details overlooked by many, including myself.

Instead of being leaders who put our heads in the sand and don't want to ever consider the timing of His coming again, may we be like the men of Issachar who had understanding of the times and knew what Israel ought to do (I Chr. 12:32). The Lord's ministers should seek to have this same understanding so their flocks might know what they should do. One thing we urgently need to do is to seek the Lord as never before! May we be so moved by the urgency of the hour, and our need to be prepared for the Lord's coming, that our words and messages would never cease to be seasoned with the prophetic message.

God's people need the prophetic message He has given us in His Word.

There must be a reason why one third of the Lord's words and messages in the Bible are related to the last days. There must be a reason why the very first part of the very first message that the Holy Spirit spoke through Peter on the Day of Pentecost in Acts 2:16-21 was an extensive prophetic message about "the last days." At least part of the reason is explained in Proverbs 29:18a: *"Where there is no vision, the people perish..."*

The Hebrew word "vision" refers to a prophetic vision, and some translations accurately translate the second part of this verse as, "The people cast off restraint." So, this verse could be translated as, "Where there is no prophetic vision, the people cast off restraint." Any pastor who has chosen to protect himself against further embarrassment and humiliation by avoiding the prophetic message will one day discover that his people have gone into a spiritual sleep. They will begin to set their eyes and hearts on this world and forget why we are on earth, and that the Lord is at the door.

It can be shown biblically that all the mistakes God's people, the Jews, made in the first coming will now be repeated by God's people, the "Gentile Church," in the second coming. (My use of the term "Gentile Church" is in reference to all born-again believers, the vast majority of whom are Gentiles presently.) A study of this is outside the scope of this book, but one example is the present reluctance of the spiritual leaders of the Church to consider the time of His coming. "The year 2000 debacle" has set us up for this. Many no longer want to even consider the prophetic message, and they have even less desire to search intently (as the prophets did) to know the time of His coming. Just as ignorance of the time of His first coming resulted in great sorrow for the Jews, so too, ignorance of the time of His second coming will bring great sorrow to many Christians. The Lord is no respecter of persons. The way He tests His Jewish people will not be more severe than the way He tests His Gentile people.

Chapter 3

The Kingdom of Heaven in the Last Days

The sheer volume of Scripture dedicated to explaining the last days reveals the importance the Lord places on this subject. It is also revealed by the Lord's reaction to the desire of His disciples to understand the end. In Matthew 24:3, they asked Him to explain the last days to them. Instead of avoiding the subject, or telling them they really did not need to understand those things, Jesus launched into one of the longest and most detailed discourses of His entire ministry. At the end of His discourse, He revealed some extremely important secrets about the end and His coming that most of us have overlooked. For many, these secrets will help clarify what happened in the year 2000, or rather, what did *not* happen and why He did not return at that time (in spite of so much evidence telling us He would). We will discover that these truths are also revealed in other Scriptures.

At the very end of Matthew 24, Jesus explains the following:

> *But and if that evil servant shall say in his heart, My lord delayeth his coming; and shall begin to smite his fellowservants, and to eat and drink with the drunken; the lord of that servant shall come in a day when he looketh not for him, and in an hour that he is not aware of, and shall cut him asunder, and appoint him his portion with the hypocrites: there shall be weeping and gnashing of teeth.* (Matt. 24:48-51)

The servant referred to here begins to yield himself to his fleshly appetites because he has concluded that the Lord is delaying His coming (the context is the second coming of Christ). This servant loses his love for his brethren and smites them. Just a few verses earlier, speaking of the last days, the Lord warned that "because iniquity shall abound, the love of many shall wax cold" (Matt. 24:12). Is it possible that the Lord is now showing us that this will occur, at least in part, because of a delay?

The basis for the evil servant's statement regarding his Lord's delay is not immediately evident. It is not clear if the Lord is, in fact, delaying His coming or if this is merely what this evil servant incorrectly concludes. Either way, this servant now believes that he has sufficient time to safely enjoy the pleasures of sin for a season since the Lord's coming has been delayed. However, the Lord continues His endtime discourse in Matthew 25 and clarifies whether there will actually be a delay or if the idea of a delay is merely a misconception of the evil servant.

Many theologians rightfully emphasize the importance of the Lord's discourse in Matthew 24 for all who want to understand the end. But His discourse on the last days does not end there. If we do not read the remainder of His endtime discourse we will miss a very important truth. He continues speaking about the end in Matthew 25:1-13 and reveals if there will actually be a delay in His coming or if this is merely the evil servant's mistaken perception.

1 Then shall the kingdom of heaven be likened unto ten virgins, which took their lamps, and went forth to meet the bridegroom.

2 And five of them were wise, and five were foolish.

3 They that were foolish took their lamps, and took no oil with them:

4 But the wise took oil in their vessels with their lamps.

5 While the bridegroom tarried, they all slumbered and slept.

6 And at midnight there was a cry made, Behold, the bridegroom cometh; go ye out to meet him.

7 Then all those virgins arose, and trimmed their lamps.

8 And the foolish said unto the wise, Give us of your oil; for our lamps are gone out.

9 But the wise answered, saying, Not so; lest there be not enough for us and you: but go ye rather to them that sell, and buy for yourselves.

10 And while they went to buy, the bridegroom came; and they that were ready went in with him to the marriage: and the door was shut.

11 Afterward came also the other virgins, saying, Lord, Lord, open to us.

12 But he answered and said, Verily I say unto you, I know you not.

13 Watch therefore, for ye know neither the day nor the hour wherein the Son of man cometh.

It is easy to ignore the little words in a biblical passage, but sometimes those little words provide a key to understanding the message. Note that the above passage begins with the word "then," meaning "at that time," as the New International Version correctly translates it. To what time is the Lord referring? The context is found in the last verses of Matthew 24 and includes, 1) the time of His coming, 2) the time when an evil servant yields himself to sin because he thinks that the Lord is delaying His coming.

Jesus explains that the ten virgins represent the Kingdom of heaven, so this is a revelation of what will happen in the Kingdom at the time of the second coming. Those who are part of that Kingdom will go forth to meet the bridegroom. From verse 10, we know they were waiting for Him to come and take them to the marriage, obviously an endtime event. But the Lord makes an amazing statement in verse 5: *"While the bridegroom tarried, they all slumbered and slept."* The Greek word translated as "tarried" here is the same Greek word translated as "delayeth" in Matthew 24:48 where the evil servant said, *"My lord delayeth his coming."* The New American Standard correctly translates verse 5 as, *"Now while the bridegroom was delaying..."*

Here, Jesus gives the answer to our uncertainty about the declaration of the evil servant regarding a delay. In the parable of the ten virgins, the Lord reveals that there will be a delay in His coming at the time when the Kingdom people go out to receive the Bridegroom. The virgins react to His delay by slumbering and sleeping. The evil servant reacts by losing his brotherly love and by living for the flesh. Therefore, when the evil servant concludes, "My Lord delays His coming," this is not a misconception but a fact that the evil servant is simply acknowledging. He is not evil because he recognizes a delay; he is evil because he yields to evil passions during the delay. So, the Lord *is*, in fact, seen to be delaying His coming in both of these parables.

Six Essential Truths Found in the Parable of the Ten Virgins

Truth One: All the virgins are symbolic of born-again Christians. Some say that only five were really born again. However, Jesus says that all ten represent the Kingdom, and a person can neither see nor enter the Kingdom if they are not born again (John 3:3, 5). Although they all had oil, the five foolish ones did not have *enough* oil. Oil is a biblical symbol of the Holy Spirit (I Sam. 16:13); even the foolish virgins had a measure of the Holy Spirit. They all had lamps. In other words, they all had light, symbolic of the gospel and of the Word of God (II Cor. 4:4-6; Psa. 119:105). They all went out to meet the bridegroom, expecting to marry Him. Only Christians are called to marry the Lord. They are all virgins. This is symbolic of a person who is not found following after other loves in this life when the Bridegroom comes.

The basis on which some students of the Word assume that five virgins are not true believers is that at the end of this parable the Lord says to them, "I do not know you." Matthew 1:25 tells us that Joseph did not "know" Mary until after Jesus was born. That is, he did not have an intimate love relationship with her. Maybe this is what is lacking in the five foolish virgins. John tells us, *"And hereby we do know that we know him, if we keep his commandments"*(I Jn. 2:3). Maybe the foolish virgin's lack of knowledge of God isn't because they are not saved, but rather because they are not obedient disciples. Either way, it seems somewhat inconsistent to disregard all the symbols of the Christian life associated with these virgins based on one phrase, the meaning of which is not certain.

Truth Two: Jesus begins this parable by saying, *"At that time the Kingdom of heaven will be like ten virgins."* As we have seen, the "time" to which Jesus refers here is the time of His coming. Consequently, what happens in this parable will be fulfilled in the last days.

Truth Three: The wise virgins took extra oil, while the foolish virgins took only the oil that was in their lamps (Matt. 25:3-4).

Truth Four: Obviously, the virgins thought they knew the approximate time of the Lord's coming because the foolish virgins had enough oil in their lamps to last until the time that they thought He would come. They had no lack of oil up to the point of the bridegroom's delay in coming. The delay is what exposed their lack of oil.

Truth Five: After it became apparent that the bridegroom was delaying His coming, all ten virgins slumbered and slept.

Truth Six: The principal mistake of the foolish virgins was not that they initially failed to take enough oil with them; they could have bought more oil at any time. They apparently had money, and there was oil for sale (v. 9-10). Their mistake was that they did not pay the price for more oil while they still had time. Who among us does not need more of the Lord's presence (oil)? But how many of us are making the same mistake these virgins made? Instead of taking advantage of the Lord's delay to pay the price for more oil, they all slumbered and slept. Their lack of oil then became a problem when they were awakened by the sudden midnight call. To their sorrow, the coming of the bridegroom was at hand and their lamps were going out. Tragically, they could have been ready for the coming of the bridegroom, but now it was too late. This parable is an admonition to all believers that just because we are part of the Kingdom through the new birth does not necessarily mean we will be ready for His coming.

An Important Observation

We can never say that someone is delaying their coming if we have no idea about an original arrival time. If a friend of mine tells me that he is going to come and visit me some day, without telling me when, it would not be logical for me to declare at 10:00 a.m. tomorrow morning that he is delaying his arrival. However, if he told me that he would arrive at my house tomorrow at 9:00 a.m., then, if he has not arrived by 10:00 a.m., I could logically declare that he is delaying his coming. According to Matthew 24:48, in the last days some will say, "My Lord delays His coming." This gives a strong implication that some will have at least an approximate idea of when the Lord is supposed to come.

The Lord reinforces this implication by giving the parable of the ten virgins immediately after the parable of the evil servant. It is reinforced because the virgins actually go out to meet the bridegroom, expecting Him to come on a specific day and apparently thinking in terms of a specific hour also. According to this parable the virgins themselves believe they know the day and approximate hour of His coming. No one would go out of their house to meet someone, expecting to spend days or weeks waiting outside. Of course, because of the Lord's delay their expectations were not met, and the Lord ended the parable saying that no one knows the day nor the hour. This does not negate other Scriptures which tell us we should discern the approximate time of His coming (I Thess. 4:16 - 5:1; Matt. 16:2-3).

The amount of oil the foolish virgins had also shows that the virgins thought they knew the time of His coming. They had enough oil to reach the hour they understood to be the hour of His coming; they did not lack oil until after the bridegroom delayed his coming. The main conclusion the Lord Himself gives to this parable is, *"Watch therefore, for ye know neither the day nor the hour wherein the Son of man cometh."* This indicates that the day and hour of His coming is precisely what the virgins thought they knew, but they had not considered the possibility of a delay.

Once a divine delay is factored into the equation, no one can know the day or hour of His coming!

What the Lord does *not* say in the main conclusion He gives to this parable is also an indication that the virgins thought they knew the time of His coming. There is no hint here that the Lord is rebuking the virgins for going out to meet Him, believing that He would come at a specific time. Rather, the more evident lesson we learn by comparing this parable with the conclusion that the Lord draws from it, is that even if we have understanding of the times, the Lord is sovereign and can choose to delay.

When someone chooses to delay their arrival, we have no way of knowing when they will actually come. If the Lord chooses to make a divine appointment and even gives us an idea of the time of His coming through understanding of the divine calendar, He can still choose to delay His coming. Once He does so, we can no longer know "the day nor hour wherein the Son of man cometh." But may we be found waiting for Him with our lamps burning when He does come!

Some may conclude that the delay in the Lord's coming, mentioned twice in Matthew 24 and 25, is simply referring to the 2,000-year delay that has already occurred. This does not fit with several details. First, the man who says that the Lord is delaying His coming and then gives himself to sinful living is suddenly cut asunder by the Lord at His coming. In its fullest sense and in the context of the last days, this must be fulfilled in people who are alive when the Lord returns, people who have stopped waiting and stopped living for Him because of the disappointment or frustration His delay has caused in their hearts. The Lord concludes the parable of the evil servant in the same way He concludes the parable of the ten virgins, saying that the Lord comes *"in a day when he looketh not for him, and in an hour that he is not aware of..."* (Matt. 24:50). Throughout Matthew 24 and 25, He uses this phrase to refer to a specific endtime event—the second coming.

There is little or no evidence in these parables to support the idea that the Lord is referring to a general 2,000-year delay. The concept of going out to meet the bridegroom on a specific day simply requires too much speculation to apply it to a 2,000-year wait. As we observed, the little word "then" with which the Lord begins this parable proves that He is revealing what will happen to those who belong to the Kingdom at the time of His coming. At the end of their wait, the virgins in this parable are brought to the marriage between Christ and His Bride. This precludes the possibility that these two parables are referring to what has happened during the last 2,000 years of general delay. This will be fulfilled only in the last days, just as all evil servants will be surprised by the sudden coming of the Lord only in the last days.

We will look at additional Scriptures that point us to a delay in the Lord's coming that most of us did not take into consideration before the year 2000. In fact, I do not know one believer, including myself, who fully grasped before the year 2000 what these Scriptures were telling us. For many Christians that delay has caused great confusion, sorrow, disappointment... even unbelief. May the fresh understanding presented in this book inspire in all of us a fresh desire to look for and patiently wait for the Lord's coming.

In the next chapter, we will consider in more detail some lessons from the parable of the ten virgins. There, I will share how the Lord brought this parable to life in an astounding way through an event experienced by a small group of pastors.

Chapter 4

Our Light Goes Out Where There Is a Lack of Oil

About three years ago, the Lord provided a retreat center for the fellowship of pastors that I oversee. Our first pastoral retreat was planned for July 2000. Although we were able to finish the construction of the buildings in time for the retreat, the electric company had not yet connected the electrical power to the property. We were able to go ahead with the retreat despite this because the Lord provided a nice diesel generator through a faithful brother. Before our meetings began, we used the generator for about 100 hours to provide power for the final preparations. It proved to be a wonderful machine! During that entire 100-hour period, it did not burn a drop of oil. We were sure it would provide all the trouble-free power necessary for as long as we would need it.

By the time our first retreat began, it seemed very unlikely to any of the pastors in our fellowship that the Lord would return in the year 2000. There were certain biblical prophecies related to His coming that had not yet been fulfilled. I knew that not only the pastors who gathered for the retreat were looking for answers, but so were their congregations. I don't think any of us were afraid of losing our ministries through being abandoned by our congregations, but we were looking for answers for them and for ourselves.

We were not afraid of losing our congregations for two reasons. First, we were not clinging to our ministries, so how could we be afraid of losing them? Second, most of the members of our congregations knew that none of us were guilty of wild, irresponsible speculations about the last days; we were not trying to be purveyors of some new thing. They knew that we were men who loved the Lord and who had a sincere love for the truth and a desire to understand God's

Word. Most of them also knew that there was strong evidence for what we had taught them. The question was not, "What will we tell the people so they won't abandon us?" Rather, the question was, "What will we tell the many seeking hearts who expected the Lord to come this year, and who are now disappointed, not because we were wrong but because the One Whom we have longed to be with for so many years has not come?"

For all of us, the issue was not the loss of our ministries nor our congregations. The issue was to receive greater understanding from the Lord and to see where we missed it so that the prophetic vision would not die in the hearts of God's people. The Apostle Paul explains that we are the "household of God" or His "holy temple," and that we are *"built upon the foundation of the apostles and prophets..."* (Eph. 2:19-21). In other words, part of the very foundation to our spiritual lives is the prophetic ministry. And *"If the foundations be destroyed, what can the righteous do?"* (Psa. 11:3). Such is the paramount importance of the prophetic message. That's why the Lord has dedicated about one third of the Bible to the prophetic message and the last days. As we saw in Proverbs, *"... without a vision the people perish,"* but *with* a vision, people are moved to run after God, as the Lord told Habakkuk: *"Write the vision, and make it plain upon tables, that he may run that readeth it"* (Hab. 2:2).

In spite of what Paul wrote in Ephesians, some may say, "I don't believe that the foundation of the Church is the apostolic and prophetic ministries. Christ is the foundation of the Church!" Yes, Christ *is* the foundation of the Church, but both Paul and Jesus taught us that there is a foundation laid upon *the* Foundation, which is Christ. For example, Jesus taught that when a wise man builds a house, he digs deeply and finds the Rock and then lays his foundation on the Rock (Lk. 6:48). That Rock or Foundation is Christ, but what is the foundation that is laid on the Rock? Paul tells us that it is apostles and prophets. A person who has no prophetic vision to run after will end up not running at all. During the retreat in July 2000, one of my deep concerns was that neither the pastors nor their sheep would lose their prophetic vision, or worse yet, lose even the desire to understand God's prophetic message.

The Lord had already begun to speak to me from the parable of the ten virgins. I felt that this message was what I should share in the very first meeting of our very first retreat. I want to share here a summary of that message I spoke to the pastors that night:

It is now easy for you or your sheep to say, 'Well, Brother Marvin was clearly wrong about the timing of the Lord's coming.' That may be true, but if I was wrong, then you were wrong also. You were wrong to not seek the Lord and hear from Him in order to know that you were being deceived. He could have told you that I was wrong. Then, you would not have been wrong in believing what I taught you. We are *all responsible* to be like the Bereans and search the Scriptures to see if what we receive from others is true. We all need to draw near to the Lord and know His mind and heart and not merely be led by what other people think or even receive from the Lord.

One of the great dangers at this point in our lives would be to end up making the same mistake that the five foolish virgins made. They did not have enough oil in their lives, and they waited too long to pay the price for more oil. They did not have enough of the oil of His presence to keep their lights burning. That oil comes upon our lives from the Holy Spirit or the presence of God as we enter into an intimate love relationship with Him. Their lights were going out. They were losing their vision. If the Lord does not come in the year 2000, will you lose your spiritual vision because you did not have a deep enough relationship with the Lord to accept a delay and still trust and seek Him?

Oh yes, they had enough oil to keep their vision burning brightly up until the time they *thought* the bridegroom would come. But when He didn't come, their lights began to go out. They even wanted to keep their lights burning by using the oil of the other virgins. A mistake that we all make at times is to live off the anointing and vision of others. Has your light and vision depended on the relationship that other believers have experienced with the Lord, including Marvin Byers, or has your vision depended on what you have personally received from the Lord? The source of our anointing and vision is becoming more evident in all of our lives in this hour when it seems that the Lord is delaying His coming.

What if the Lord had not delayed His coming in this parable? The lack of oil in the lives of the foolish virgins would never have been revealed. No one would have ever noticed. They would have entered into the Marriage with a serious lack in their lives, and maybe they would not have even been aware of it themselves. Will a delay in His coming cause our own spiritual lack to be revealed, including our shallow relationship with the Lord? Can our own spiritual vision endure a divine delay beyond the year 2000? Is our own relationship with Him deep enough to accept things we don't understand, without losing our hope, our vision, and our love for Him?

On the other hand, if there has been shallowness in our relationship with the Lord, would it not be a great act of mercy for Him to delay His coming, giving us a little more time to prepare? I would ask all of us, If the Lord were to come now, would we be ready for the Marriage, or, with great sorrow, would we hear Him say, 'I do not know you?'

If your lights are going out because of a lack of oil, causing you to lose your vision, it is time to awake from sleep and pay the price for more oil. It is time to draw near to the Lord and enter into a deeper love relationship with Him where the anointing oil of His Spirit rests upon us and gives us ever greater light and understanding.

On the first night of our pastoral retreat, we concluded the meeting as planned at about 10:00 p.m. We all went to our rooms and prepared for bed. Then at 10:30 p.m., a very disconcerting silence fell over the entire property of several acres. The noise of the generator that could be heard far off in the distance stopped abruptly. To some it must have been a sweet silence when that noise was replaced by the sound of the crickets.

My first thought was that everyone would be anxious about why the generator had stopped running; then I realized that no one would be alarmed, since they would all think that our plan was to turn off the generator each night after everyone had retired. Besides, I thought, the problem was mechanical, and we wouldn't be able to fix it until morning. Surely something had broken. I knew it could not be a lack of oil, since the engine didn't burn any. It couldn't have been a lack of fuel since the 40-hour tank had been filled that afternoon. As I further considered the matter, I realized we would have no water for showers in the morning because the water pumps were electric.

I decided to call Brother Eddie, our maintenance supervisor, a loving brother and faithful servant, who was likely already in bed at his home in the city. As always, his cheerful response was, "I'll be right there." I was in and out of sleep while I waited for him to arrive. At one point I was somewhere between consciousness and sleep when I thought I heard him arriving. However, it sounded like he was driving a Mack truck. In my sleepy and beclouded thoughts I said to myself, "I didn't know that Eddie had such a big truck." With that thought I awoke with a start, only to realize that the sound of the "Mack truck" was coming from our neighbor's room. What a trial for all the wives, including my own, who have to endure the snoring of their husbands, especially when it sounds like a Mack truck!

I was still half-awake when Eddie arrived around midnight. I went out to see if I could be of any assistance in discovering the problem. Words can hardly describe our amazement when we discovered that during the previous six hours the generator had burned six quarts of oil; it had stopped because of a lack of oil. To put this in perspective, that is approximately the equivalent of a car burning a quart every 50 miles! We would have to add a quart of oil about six or seven times between every tank of gas. I was convinced that the engine was totally ruined. That's what usually happens when an engine runs out of oil.

I said to Eddie, "Well, please get the oil. Let's see what happens if we fill it and start it again. Maybe we can limp along for the three remaining days of the retreat with a ruined engine." It was then that Eddie explained to me that there was only a little more than a quart of oil on the property. "Since this engine never burned oil," he said, "we just never thought to buy any extra." So a few minutes past midnight, Eddie and I got into his truck and headed off to the city, a twenty-minute ride one way. As we went out through the gates of the property, I prayed, "Lord, why is this happening? I have a full day tomorrow with all these pastors, and here I am spending a good part of the night trying to buy oil and fill the generator."

We found an open gas station and returned with the oil around 1:00am. We added six quarts of oil and started the engine. It sounded fine and worked perfectly through the rest of the night. The next morning I was still in a spiritual fog. I had not received understanding of what had happened the night before. I probably did what we all do so often—ask the Lord questions and then fail to wait for the answers. Fortunately, each of us is only one member in the Body, and the other members can help us out when we are totally blind, deaf, and dumb—my normal condition without divine intervention.

The generator was purring along just fine when I went down for breakfast. I casually mentioned to one of the pastors about what had taken place, and his immediate response was, "Isn't it amazing? The very thing you shared with us last night was what happened a few minutes later—the lights went out because of a lack of oil." It was as though the Lord put a trumpet to my deaf ear to cause me to hear His message! My brother did not need to say another word. The message came flooding into my soul all at once. Yes, not only were the lights of the virgins going out for lack of oil, but also it was after the midnight call that they went out to buy oil! Unfortunately, it was too late. The bridegroom came while they were gone to buy it. Eddie and I had gone out through the gates to buy oil at precisely ten minutes after midnight.

I knew the Lord was speaking to all of us, but I also knew He was especially trying to get my attention. Up to this point, I had no idea to what lengths the Lord had gone to get our attention. It wasn't until days later that I fully understood what an incredible miracle the Lord had done to cause an otherwise perfect engine to burn six quarts of oil in six hours. You see, the engine never burned oil like that again. Until this day, almost three years later, it burned oil like that on only one occasion—during the very hours I was speaking on the loss of our spiritual light and vision caused by the lack of oil, and our great need to buy oil before we hear the midnight call.

As the Lord's message flooded in upon me, He spoke two key thoughts. The first thing He said was, "I have done this miracle to show you why I am delaying My coming. My people [and I knew He was including me] are not ready for the Wedding. Most do not have enough oil and their lights are going out. They are losing their vision, and are all slumbering and sleeping. I am giving you time to pay the price to buy the oil before it is too late."

For many of us, the reason we have not paid the price for more oil is much the same reason why Eddie had not bought more oil for the generator—we didn't need it. After all, the generator had no problems. It was such a good machine that it did not burn oil. In the lives of millions of Christians, everything has been going along just fine. We feel no need to draw near to the Lord to obtain more of His presence in our lives. Life has been good. There are many enjoyable things on which to spend our time. After all, we don't want to get out of balance and become too spiritually minded. The world has many very entertaining things for us to do; our spiritual life isn't everything, you know.

May God do whatever He must do to take away our spiritual contentedness, even if it means bringing problems to our lives. May He deliver us from being at ease in Zion (Amos 6:1). Oh, that the urgency of the hour might grip our hearts! Among other things, maybe the Lord is allowing Islamic superterrorism to motivate us all to seek Him more fervently.

The second thought that He spoke to me is that He is not sadistic. He did not do such an amazing miracle on a man-made machine simply to tell us that we have a problem but that it's too late to do anything about it. In His great tenderness and mercy, He said to me, "I am giving you this message in such a clear way because I want you to know that there is still time to buy the oil and to be ready for the Wedding day. There is still hope for My people, but there is no time to waste."

At that moment, I knew He was calling Barbara and me, personally, to spend more time with Him and less time in everything else, including public ministry. What we did, personally, is not what He is calling everyone to do, nor would it be possible, but neither is it necessary for everyone. Shortly after this experience, my wife and I left our full-time ministry, rented an apartment, and dedicated ourselves full-time to seeking the Lord. We continue to do so, but we are now also including ministerial trips on our calendar. We want to continue seeking the Lord, but we also want to do what we can to be a blessing to others, encouraging people to look up. Our redemption draws near! Let's not lose our vision, nor our love, for His coming just because He did not come when many of us "went out to meet Him."

Chapter 5

A Very Costly Delay

From time to time throughout history God has executed judgments upon individuals or groups of people that seemed uniquely severe and unusually harsh. It still seems that way today, as we read about them in the Bible, especially if we view those judgments from man's perch instead of from God's throne. Although some judgments were executed on vile sinners, others were executed on seemingly very little mistakes of very righteous men. The judgments were so severe that they not only caught the attention of the generation living at the time, but every generation since. In fact, the very purpose of those judgments was, and still is, to catch our attention.

Those judgments served one of two divine purposes.

Purpose One: In some cases, the Lord wanted to establish indelible benchmarks of history so that all of humanity would forever understand His wrath against specific types of sin. We should all heed His warning shots across the bows of our spiritual ships. Those impressive judgments were not a demonstration of unbridled divine anger that fell by sheer chance upon some hapless soul. Nor were they meted out in a biased manner just because God took a disliking to someone. Rather, through them He was giving us a point of reference by which we would understand the consequences of certain sins or mistakes. In His mercy, He was shouting to humanity, "This is the end of *every* unrepentant person who walks on this path, not just the end of a few people whose judgments are recorded in My Word. Though you may not face this judgment today, you, too, will surely face it eternally if you do not repent." Being a merciful God, His desire is for every person to repent and be saved. In His great mercy, He is willing to do everything He can to reach that goal, even if it means sending unusually harsh judgments on a few people to show many people what all unrepentant sinners will face.

I am not merely speculating that this message is in God's heart. Jesus declared precisely this thought regarding two tragic judgments in The Gospel of Luke. Although the judgments mentioned by Jesus may or may not have been *instituted* by God, they certainly were *allowed* by God; He then used them to give mankind a message. Luke 13:1-5 tells us:

> *There were present at that season some that told him of the Galilaeans, whose blood Pilate had mingled with their sacrifices. And Jesus answering said unto them, Suppose ye that these Galilaeans were sinners above all the Galilaeans, because they suffered such things? I tell you, Nay: but, except ye repent, ye shall all likewise perish. Or those eighteen, upon whom the tower in Siloam fell, and slew them, think ye that they were sinners above all men that dwelt in Jerusalem? I tell you, Nay: but, except ye repent, ye shall all likewise perish.*

Purpose Two: There is a second purpose for the seemingly harsh judgments found in God's Word. Few things catch our attention so abruptly when reading the Bible as a seemingly harsh or seemingly unfair judgment on someone. We are almost forced to ask, "Why?" The Word can give us the answers as we meditate on what was involved. Those judgments stand as signposts to point us toward a goal and to keep us on the right path to reach that goal. In other words, there are certain truths and lessons so near and dear to the heart of God that He chose to punctuate them with a severe judgment on someone who failed in that area. Again, He did so in mercy, desiring that we would take heed to another's mistake and not end up doing the same. Once again, He shows no partiality. The judgment on one person for a given mistake will end up being the judgment on all of us who make that mistake unless we repent and turn from our own ways.

The judgment on Sodom is a classic example of God revealing His wrath against a specific sin or way of life. The Lord revealed to humanity in very clear terms His attitude toward Sodomy or homosexuality. All who continue to walk in that sin will ultimately experience the fire of God's judgment against them (as surely as Sodom did). Romans 1:32 confirms this in the context of the homosexuality and lesbianism found in Romans 1:26-27. Peter confirms that Sodom's judgment was *"an example to those who afterward would live ungodly"* (II Pet. 2:6, NKJV).

The judgment that Elisha brought on 42 children who mocked him revealed in a tragic way how much God hates mocking (II Ki. 2:23-24). Proverbs 17:5a tells us, *"Whoso mocketh the poor reproacheth his Maker."* And Proverbs 30:17 warns, *"The eye that mocketh at his father, and despiseth to obey his mother, the ravens of the valley shall pick it out, and the young eagles shall eat it."* Most of us know by experience just how deep a wound mocking can leave in our hearts. Mocking hurts even if it comes from children, but how much more it cuts when it comes from our equals or, worse yet, from those over us—our parents, our boss, our spiritual leaders, etc.

Two times fire literally came out of the Tabernacle of God and consumed people. The first time was when Nadab and Abihu offered strange fire before the Lord (Lev. 10:1-2). The second was when God's fire consumed 250 men who had sided with Korah in his rebellion against Moses. They were all consumed as they offered incense before the Lord. In both cases, God was showing us that no one should attempt to draw near to the Lord on their own terms, using their own devices and methods. Nor should anyone presume to appoint himself to the ministry.

We all know that Lot's wife turned into a pillar of salt. In case we have not meditated sufficiently on that severe judgment while reading the Old Testament, the New Testament encourages us to do so when it exhorts us to "remember Lot's wife" (Lk. 17:32). Her mistake was a very common mistake in the lives of parents. She was looking back, in disobedience to God, because her children were more important to her than God and His commandments.

Some believe that Lot's wife was looking back at the things she was leaving behind. It is true that a love of the world may have been part of the reason she looked back. However, we are told that the night before Lot fled with his wife and two virgin daughters, he had warned his sons-in-law of the coming horrific judgment (Gen. 19:14). Apparently, Lot had at least two daughters already married to Sodomites. What a temptation for any mother! The tug on the strings of her heart was simply too strong for Lot's wife to obey God's commandment to not look back (Gen. 19:17). For many parents, their children occupy the first place in their lives. If this is not corrected, the day will come (and we are very close to that moment) when parents find themselves in rebellion against the Lord's will by putting their children first in a critical moment of decision.

In light of what was involved, one of the most awesome judgments of God is the one that came on a man so righteous as Moses. As few men in history have done, he faithfully followed the Lord for almost 120 years. He endured a harsh life in the wilderness for 80 years because of his love for the Lord and His people. His first 40 years were spent pastoring sheep because he chose the Lord's way and the afflictions of God's people rather than enjoy a life of sin in Egypt. Then, after another 40 years of leading God's people through the wilderness, the time finally came to enter into the Promised Land. Surely, his heart was ecstatic with joy at the thought of it!

However, when Moses made the seemingly small mistake of smiting the rock twice instead of speaking to the rock, the Lord told him that he would not be permitted to enter the land. Though Moses pleaded with the Lord, the Lord was adamant and would not allow him to enter nor even speak to Him again about the matter (Deut. 3:26). Imagine! After living for 120 years with a longing to enter into the Promised Land that God had promised Abraham, he is now excluded from it all because of one small mistake.

What is the lesson? I leave that to the reader to decide. Obviously, the Lord wants us to meditate on the message that this judgment gives us, but we cannot do justice to the enormity of that lesson here. Such a catastrophic judgment on such a seemingly little thing in the life of a man of unrivaled spirituality is certainly meant to call our attention to a *very* important message!

Another absolutely astounding judgment is that which came on King Saul for his seemingly small mistake. It should be considered astounding not only for its severity, but also in the light of God's dealings with the next king of Israel—King David (in II Samuel 11-12). David committed adultery and then murdered Uriah the Hittite, a very faithful servant who had followed David through his long ordeal in the wilderness, as he fled from Saul. After confronting David with his sin, Nathan the prophet immediately told him that God had forgiven his sin.

Let's compare this with what happened in Saul's life. The prophet Samuel was one of the most godly men in biblical history. He revealed the heart, nature and character of the Lord like few other men of God. The Bible never mentions any failure or sin that God found in the personal life of Samuel. In many ways, he was a man after God's own heart. Maybe that is why he was called to anoint and call David to be king, the man of whom the Lord would later say, "*He is a man after My own heart*' (Acts 13:22, NKJV).

One day, Samuel told Saul to go to Gilgal and wait seven days, then he would come to him there. The Bible tells us that Saul *"tarried seven days, according to the set time that Samuel had appointed: but Samuel came not to Gilgal..."* (I Sam. 13:8). Then, Saul took an animal and offered a burnt offering to God on an altar. When Samuel finally came, he asked Saul why he had done so. Saul's response was:

> *Because I saw that the people were scattered from me, and that thou camest not within the days appointed... I forced myself therefore, and offered a burnt offering.* (I Sam. 13:11-12)

If it weren't for Samuel's reaction to this, few would consider this to be a decisive moment in the life of Saul. But Samuel's reaction gives us conclusive evidence that the Lord is shouting to us here about an extremely important issue. David's murder and adultery were forgiven by Nathan the prophet, but what was Samuel the prophet's message to Saul for his seemingly small offense?

> *And Samuel said to Saul, Thou hast done foolishly: thou hast not kept the commandment of the LORD thy God, which he commanded thee: for now would the LORD have established thy kingdom upon Israel for ever. But now thy kingdom shall not continue: the LORD hath sought him a man after his own heart...* (I Sam. 13:13-14a).

Three stark realities are recorded in this passage:

1) Samuel said he would come at a certain time, and he did not come at that time. Are we to assume that at this moment Samuel was moving in the flesh and that he had failed the Lord and Saul? Had he been delayed by a real emergency or merely by a lack of punctuality? Or is it possible that even in this issue of a delay in his coming Samuel was under the guidance of God's Spirit? Is it possible that he was revealing another aspect of the character of God—that God might also set a time for His coming and then delay His coming to test our hearts?

2) Saul faithfully waited for Samuel's arrival right up to the last minute of time designated for Samuel's arrival. Saul did not fail to wait. Rather, it was after waiting that he failed to respond properly to the delay in Samuel's coming. When faced with a delay, he was more concerned about losing the people than he was about pleasing the Lord. Therefore, he acted foolishly and manifested unbelief by disobeying.

Unbelief manifests itself in at least two ways. It causes us to depart from God (Heb. 3:12), and it causes us to disobey, as Saul did and Israel had done before him (Heb. 3:17-19).

3) Saul lost his kingdom and his place in God when he did not respond properly to a delay. His attitude and actions when faced with a delay were displeasing to the Lord. Some would quickly point out, and rightfully so, that a major issue here is that Saul was not a priest and so he had no right to offer sacrifices. However, Saul's problem in this biblical account did not begin with his sin of attempting to usurp the priesthood. He had not done that at any time during the seven-day wait. He did so in response to a delay and the fact that the people were abandoning him. His wrong response to a delay was his first mistake, not the specific sin that he ended up committing (he could just as easily have done some other foolish thing with the same ultimate judgment).

Because of the words of Jesus, we are forced to reject the thought that the main issue here was the usurping of the exclusive rights of the priesthood. David usurped one of the rights that belonged exclusively to the priesthood and was not even rebuked for it. He ate the shewbread:

> *Have ye not read what David did... how he entered into the house of God, and did eat the shewbread, which was not lawful for him to eat, neither for them which were with him, but only for the priests?* (Matt. 12:3b-4)

Since usurping the priesthood in a given moment is not the unforgivable sin, we must assume that there is a deeper message in Saul's story than the issue of the priesthood. Not only in the issue of the priesthood, but in other issues as well, the contrast between God's dealing with Saul and His dealing with David is astounding. David was forgiven for adultery and murder while Saul lost his kingdom because he did not handle a delay properly. Is this merely a case of extreme divine partiality, or does God want us to receive a vital message through His seemingly severe judgment on Saul? In this Bible story, a man lost his kingdom and the ministry that God had called him to for what seemed to be a small mistake. The Lord certainly wants us to meditate on this story and learn from it.

If we consider the details, a clear reason emerges for why God was not showing partiality in His dealings with David and Saul. There was one enormous difference between the two men. When Nathan confronted David with his sin, David's immediate response was to repent.

When Samuel confronted Saul with his sin, Saul's immediate response was to make excuses. The Lord is quick to forgive the repentant soul of even very serious failures like adultery and murder. On the other hand, He severely judges those who make excuses for their sin. But we are faced with some difficult doctrinal issues here. Without going into all those issues, we know that repentance is something the Lord Himself gives (Acts 5:31). Instead of giving repentance to Pharaoh, the Bible tells us that God hardened his heart (e.g., Exod. 9:12). The Lord revealed a key truth to Moses in the wilderness, explaining to him that *"He has mercy on whom He wills, and whom He wills He hardens"* (Rom. 9:18).

There are many factors related to the human heart that cause God to decide to either harden a person or give them repentance. Humility is one of the major issues; being merciful to others is another (James 4:6; Matt. 5:7). Like Esau, something in Saul's heart kept him from receiving a spirit of repentance from God in his time of testing (Heb. 12:17). The Lord knew that Saul would one day fail to repent at a crucial moment. But why would God choose that Saul's crucial moment and test revolve around a delay in the coming of His prophet? God could have chosen any number of things to expose the condition of Saul's heart and find his lack of repentance. God must have chosen this particular event because, among other lessons, He wanted to teach us about responding to delays. A valid question here is, If Saul's failure to respond properly to a delay is not one of the messages in this passage, then why did God allow a delay to be the source of Saul's test?

Certainly, Saul was not the only man in history whom God tested by allowing a delay. The Lord Himself tests each of us at times with divine delays, as most have already experienced. Maybe a word of counsel from someone who is spiritually trustworthy, like Samuel, has caused us to believe that God's answer for our situation would come within a specific time frame. Then, there was a delay in His visitation or deliverance. After all, what is patience for and how else do we learn it? Also, how deep is our love for Him if we can't handle a divine delay without losing our trust and confidence in Him? Saul revealed a lack of trust in both the Lord and Samuel in the time of delay; therefore, he responded foolishly.

Is it wise to presume that the Lord couldn't possibly delay His *final* coming to mankind in these last days? Is it not possible that God's people are being tested now in the same way Saul was tested, by a delay in His coming just before the Son of David takes the throne? If so, it is also possible that we, too, could lose our place in God by not responding properly to a delay in the coming of the greatest of all prophets, the Lord Jesus Christ. If we are, in fact, living in a time when there has been a divine delay in the second coming, will we respond properly to that delay or will we respond foolishly as Saul did?

Whether the year 2000 was actually significant on God's calendar or not, there are lessons to be learned from the various reactions of those who thought something would happen that year. Later, we will consider some of the ways in which Christians have reacted to the fact that the Lord did not come when they expected Him to come. Only one of those reactions brings joy to the Lord.

Many, if not all, of the events surrounding the lives of the biblical prophets are, in and of themselves, prophetic with a prophetic message. For example, the Lord told Ezekiel:

> *Speak unto the house of Israel, Thus saith the Lord God... Ezekiel is unto you a sign: according to all that he hath done shall ye do: and when this cometh, ye shall know that I am the Lord God.* (Ezek. 24:21-24)

Isaiah walked naked for three years to show what the Lord would do to Egypt and Ethiopia (Isa. 20:2-3). Hosea married a harlot to show the Lord's unchanging love toward Israel (Hos. 1:2; 3:1). Jeremiah wore a yoke around his neck to show that the Lord had placed the yoke of Babylon on all the nations (Jer. 27:1-8).

It seems very possible that the details surrounding the story of Samuel's delay and Saul's reaction and rejection also point prophetically to the last days. For example, Samuel's delay took place at the end of seven days. In the Book of Revelation, the number seven is intimately linked with the last days, appearing there more than 50 times. Throughout the Bible it is often linked to the end. In fact, the end of all the main periods of time that God programmed into the biblical calendar are associated with the number seven.

Man was commanded to work for six days and rest the seventh, the day that marked the end of the week. Since a day with the Lord is a thousand years (Psa. 90:4; II Pet. 3:8), the Jews have long believed that the Millennial Kingdom would come 6,000 years after Adam, giving both man and the Earth a one-thousand-year day of rest. There were seven weeks between Passover and Pentecost. There were six months between the beginning of the year and the seventh month, when the three great feasts were celebrated. The Bible refers to the seventh month as "the end of the year" (Exod. 23:16). The year of release was after seven years (Deut. 31:10), and the year of jubilee was after seven times seven years (Lev. 25:8-9).

The story of Samuel and Saul seems to refer to the time of the end for many reasons. The final outcome of this story was that David took the throne of Israel. God has given to Jesus the throne of His father, David (Lk. 1:32). David's Old Testament throne is the throne Christ inherits in the New Testament. Surely, then, as we consider David's throne—including how it began—we can learn lessons about Christ's throne. Of course, David was a prophet also, as shown by his many prophetic Psalms. Like the other Old Testament prophets, his life was surrounded with prophetic events pointing forward in time to Jesus. When Samuel rejected Saul, he said that God would seek for a man after His own heart to rule over Israel. Is there anyone who fulfills this prophetic word more than Jesus, the Son of David? Is this declaration not also prophetic?

Jesus will soon take the throne of Israel. Maybe the way David's throne began gives a prophetic message also. It began when a man who had been called to be a king lost his place in God because he responded unwisely to a delay. We are also called to be kings, but the Lord is able to keep us from losing our place in God because of reacting in unbelief if it turns out that a time of a delay is somehow a factor in His coming. It was a very costly delay for Saul. May the judgment he received teach us God's way so that we do not repeat his very costly mistake in these last days!

Chapter 6

There Will Be No More Delay!

Other Scriptures seem to tell us that there will be a divine delay just before the Lord returns. One indicates that the delay occurs precisely before the resurrection and rapture. Once again, no one can reasonably say that a person has delayed his arrival if no time has been established for that arrival. We have already seen that in the parable of the ten virgins they *did* have understanding of when the bridegroom was going to come. They went out to meet Him, but He delayed in coming.

During thousands of years, many Jews believed the Messiah would come 6,000 years after Adam's creation. The year 2000 was the approximate end of that period, according to biblical and secular history. Like the Jews, many Christians expected the year 2000 to be the time of His coming or else the beginning of the end. Could it be that they were not all wrong, but, rather, that the Lord allowed us to know the approximate time of His coming? Only by knowing this would anyone be able to say that He was delaying His coming? Before we consider the Scripture that reveals there will be a delay just before the resurrection and rapture, we need to discover where the resurrection and rapture occur in the Book of Revelation.

Paul Links the Resurrection and Rapture With the Last Trumpet of Revelation

Paul makes it clear that when the resurrection occurs, the rapture will also occur immediately afterward. In I Thessalonians 4:16-17 he writes:

For the Lord himself shall descend from heaven with a shout, with the voice of the archangel, and with the trump of God: and the dead in Christ shall rise first: then we which are alive and remain shall be caught up together with them in the clouds, to meet the Lord in the air: and so shall we ever be with the Lord.

In I Corinthians 15:51-52, Paul further explains that the resurrection (and therefore the rapture) is associated with a mystery and that it will occur at the last trump. Paul declares:

Behold, I shew you a mystery; we shall not all sleep, but we shall all be changed, in a moment, in the twinkling of an eye, at the last trump: for the trumpet shall sound, and the dead shall be raised incorruptible, and we shall be changed.

Finally, Paul gives us an additional fact about the mystery that helps us find the location of the resurrection and rapture in the Book of Revelation. He explains:

How that by revelation he made known unto me the mystery; (as I wrote afore in few words, whereby, when ye read, ye may understand my knowledge in the mystery of Christ) which in other ages was not made known unto the sons of men, as it is now revealed unto his holy apostles and prophets by the Spirit... (Eph. 3:3-5).

By comparing the above passages we find three interrelated concepts: 1) The resurrection and rapture will occur at the last trumpet; 2) the resurrection (and therefore the rapture) is related to a mystery; and 3) this mystery has been revealed to the prophets. (For anyone desiring biblical proof that Paul is referring to the same mystery in those passages, please refer to my book, *The Mystery: A Lost Key*.)

Revelation 10:7 brings these thoughts together:

But in the days of the voice of the seventh angel, when he shall begin to sound, the mystery of God should be finished, as he hath declared to his servants the prophets.

Three concepts are revealed here also: 1) the seventh angel sounds the seventh and last trumpet of Revelation; 2) a mystery is associated with that trumpet and is fulfilled here; and 3) this mystery has been revealed to the prophets. (For those desiring more proof that the rapture will occur at the seventh trumpet of Revelation, please refer to my book, *The Final Victory: The Year 2000?*, especially pages 91-163.)

Understanding that the resurrection and rapture occur in Revelation 10:7 provides further evidence that there will be a delay in the fulfillment of these events. Consider what Revelation tells us in the preceding two verses:

> *Then the angel I had seen standing on the sea and on the land raised his right hand to heaven. And he swore by him who lives for ever and ever, who created the heavens and all that is in them, the earth and all that is in it, and the sea and all that is in it, and said, There will be no more delay!* (Rev. 10:5-6, NIV)

The Greek word translated as "delay" here is the same Greek word that is used in Matthew 24:48 and Matthew 25:5, translated there as "delay" by various Bible versions. The only difference is that this passage utilizes the Greek noun while the passage in Matthew uses the verb form. The Greek word "more" in the highlighted phrase above can also be translated as "further" as it is in Matthew 26:65 (KJV, NKJV). So, for clarity, the last phrase of the verse above could be translated as "There will be no further delay."

Here we find an amazing fact. If the above translation is correct concerning the angelic declaration—"There will be no more delay"—this shows us that there has been, in fact, a delay up to that point, but there will be no further delay. The angel would not swear that "there will be no more delay" if there has been no delay at all. As soon as he makes this declaration, the resurrection and rapture occur, as seen in the next verse (Rev. 10:7).

At some point in our lives, most of us have probably assumed that the angel in Revelation 10:6 is referring to the more than 2,000-year "delay" in His return. He promised to come again and there has now been a very long *wait* for Him to come. However, there is a huge difference between the word "wait" and the word "delay." The Church has waited for His return for over 2,000 years, but that does not necessarily mean there has been a delay in His coming.

No one would doubt that the Lord has always known His own divine calendar of events, including the time He ordained for both His first and second comings. If, from the beginning, He has had a time established for His coming and He then comes at that precise time, then neither we nor an angel would ever be able to say that there has been a "delay" in His coming. We would be able to say that there has been a long "wait," but not a "delay."

If Revelation 10:6-7 were the only scriptural basis we had for believing that there might be a delay in the Lord's coming, then most would rightfully question its precise meaning. Besides, it is never wise to base any truth on one lone verse in the Bible. However, as we discovered in Chapter 3, Jesus introduced the concept of a delay in His coming in His own endtime discourse (Matt. 24:48-25:5). What we find in Revelation, therefore, is simply a confirmation of what the Lord Himself had already taught His disciples about a delay in His return during the last days.

Chapter 7

Why a Delay Is Crucial

In the pastoral retreats of our organization, I have often explained the seriousness of arriving late to a meeting. In those retreats we normally deal with subjects that must be heard and well understood by everyone. For this reason, when someone is missing at the beginning of a meeting, we do not begin until the missing person arrives. Corporate business meetings often follow the same policy. Of course, there is little choice if the tardy person is scheduled to give the presentation.

Suppose 50 people are involved in such a meeting. If a person arrives just five minutes late, he has robbed five minutes of time from the lives of 49 other people. This is a total of 245 minutes of life, the life of the others who arrived on time and had to wait for him to arrive (49 people x 5 minutes = 245 minutes). In other words, that person has been guilty of robbing from others a little over four hours of human life and productiveness. As one man I know has often said, "When I arrive late, I am telling everyone else that their time is not as important as my time. Or, that their lives are not as important as mine." Not a good message! Why then, would the Lord be late in arriving?

A Delay Gives Us More Time to Get Ready

Ironically, if the Lord delays His arrival in the second coming, He is doing just the opposite of what we do when we arrive late. He actually is giving us all a little more time, a little more life on this earth. When we step into eternity, time no longer exists, nor does the opportunity to be changed. We will have no more time to do the "good works" God has created us to do and for which we will receive a reward (Eph. 2:10 and I Tim. 6:18-19). A divine delay would be an expression of mercy, giving us more time to get ready for His appearing and ready for heaven.

Of course, more time will do us no good if we do not use it wisely.

If we are now actually in a time of divine delay, it is apparent that some are using their extra time in the wrong way, as we will see.

Over the last couple of years, I have asked many people, "Would you have been ready for the Lord's return if He had come in the year 2000?" I am sure that some Christians would quickly answer "Yes," but I have not received that answer from anyone yet. Most people I know realize that the Bride of Christ must make herself ready for the Wedding. Revelation 19:7 exhorts us:

Let us be glad and rejoice, and give honour to him: for the marriage of the Lamb is come, and his wife hath made herself ready.

As the Bride of Christ, how can we make ourselves ready? Paul gives us some very clear instructions:

And... knowing the time, that now it is high time to awake out of sleep: for now is our salvation nearer than when we believed. The night is far spent, the day is at hand: let us therefore cast off the works of darkness, and let us put on the armour of light. Let us walk honestly, as in the day; not in rioting and drunkenness, not in chambering and wantonness, not in strife and envying. But put ye on the Lord Jesus Christ, and make not provision for the flesh, to fulfil the lusts thereof. (Rom. 13:11-14)

The night is far spent and a new day is about to dawn upon the earth. Peter also refers to a glorious salvation that will be revealed in the last days (I Pet. 1:5). It will be a full and complete salvation that will save us from this world and take us to the Marriage. All of us who understand that the Lord's coming is at hand must also hear the call of the Spirit given by Paul here—*"It is high time to awake out of sleep."*

Paul explains what is involved in awaking out of sleep. We must cast off the works of darkness. He goes on to explain that this involves putting an end to the life that is lived for the desires and pleasures of the flesh. We are called to "put on Christ," not providing means by which the flesh can fulfill its earthly lusts. In Colossians 3:9-10, Paul gives us understanding of how the "new man" (Christ) obtains greater strength and vigor in our lives. He declares, *"Lie not one to another, seeing that ye have put off the old man with his deeds; and have put on the new man, which is renewed in knowledge..."* As we receive more knowledge of God and His ways, the life of Christ is strengthened within us. May we all spend much less time filling ourselves with knowledge of the ways of Hollywood and the world and choose to fill our hearts and minds with the knowledge of God that can be obtained through His Word.

Spending time in prayer brings great blessing, but spending time in the Word must accompany our prayer life. The Word is a vital part of our preparation for the Wedding, accomplishing many things in our spiritual lives. It washes us so that we will be ready for the Marriage (Eph. 5:26-27). Naomi prepared Ruth for her marriage with Boaz, and the first thing that she instructed her to do was to wash (Ru. 3:3). It is the Word that washes us.

Some claim they are too busy to spend time reading the Bible, but they have time to watch television for many hours each week. The issue is our priorities. Do we really believe that it is high time to awake out of our spiritual sleep and allow the Holy Spirit to prepare us for the Wedding? Sooner or later, every person will abandon the pleasures of this world. The pleasures of the world have no place in heaven, and they will never be enjoyed in hell. May none of us delay any longer in surrendering fully to the Lord so that we do not miss the Wedding.

May we always have enough humility to recognize that we are not yet what we should be in any area of our lives. *"Blessed are the poor in spirit: for theirs is the kingdom of heaven"* (Matt. 5:3). The Lord will provide for all our needs, but if we have no needs then we can expect no provision. He gives His grace to the humble and needy soul.

If we, as His Bride, did not make ourselves ready for the Wedding before the year 2000, wouldn't it be just like the Lord to awaken us out of our sleep now and show us that it is time for Him to come? Wouldn't the One whose name is Mercy show us that we are not ready, then also give us a little more time to correct whatever needs to be corrected and to make ourselves ready? This is precisely what He was telling us in that first pastoral retreat where the lights went out because of a lack of oil. He was telling us that we were not ready but that He, in His kindness, was giving us more time to prepare.

A Delay Gives the Scoffers
Time to Reveal Themselves

Peter wrote:

This second epistle, beloved, I now write unto you; in both which I stir up your pure minds by way of remembrance: that ye may be mindful of the words which were spoken before by the holy prophets, and of the commandment of us the apostles of the Lord and

*and Saviour: Knowing this first, that there shall come in the last
days scoffers, walking after their own lusts, and saying, Where is
the promise of his coming?...* (II Pet. 3:1-4a).

Upon careful consideration, this proves to be a very interesting statement. Note that Peter was talking about a time in the future. He said
that scoffers "would come." Peter knew he would grow old and die before the Lord returned (John 21:18-19). He was not saying here that
scoffers would arise during his lifetime, since Peter had just written
that he would soon die (II Pet. 1:14). He was talking about "the last
days." Regardless of what our concept of "the last days" might be, Peter
defined them explicitly in Acts 2:17-21:

*And it shall come to pass in the last days... I will shew wonders in
heaven above, and signs in the earth beneath; blood, and fire, and
vapour of smoke: the sun shall be turned into darkness, and the
moon into blood, before that great and notable day of the Lord come.*

Only in the last few years have we begun to experience the events
that Peter associates with the last days. Daniel 12:4 defines the last
days as a time when knowledge would increase. In 69 years, mankind
progressed from the age of the horse and buggy in 1900 to walking on
the moon in 1969. That certainly is an increase in knowledge! Few
question whether or not we are in the last days. Later, we will consider
proof that the Lord's coming is near.

Regarding Peter's reference to scoffers, two key questions should
be asked. First, were there no scoffers in Peter's day who asked why
the Lord had not fulfilled the promise of His coming? Second, weren't
scoffers always going to exist between Peter's day and the second coming? Regardless of the answers, Peter is talking here about a specific
time—the last days—and that scoffers "would come" in the future. He
is not speaking about his own time. Either the scoffers Peter mentions
are a special class of scoffers that did not exist before, or else they are
scoffing at a *specific* "promise of His coming" that would be made in
the last days, and that had not been heard before. A third option is that
both of these possibilities will prove to be true in the last days.

There are three undeniable facts that may well have something to
do with the fulfillment of Peter's prophecy.

First, there has never been a time during the last several centuries
when so many Christians and so many sectors of the Church were
openly speaking about the possibility of the Lord's coming in or around

a specific year—the year 2000. Some simply blamed it on millennial fever, perhaps because they did not read any of the convincing evidence being presented by many students and teachers of the Bible. Certainly, at no time in modern history has "the promise of His coming" been proclaimed by true Christians to the extent it was before the year 2000.

Some declare that the Church has always said that the coming of Jesus is near. Those who believe this are simply misinformed. Peter certainly did not preach that Jesus would come during his lifetime. He knew that he would grow old and die. Paul did not believe the Lord would come during his lifetime either. He was hoping to have part in the resurrection, because he also expected to die (Phil. 3:10-11; II Tim. 4:6).

Many of the founding fathers of the United States were Christians. Some were even pastors. Much of what they wrote, said, and believed is still with us today. Many of them believed that the United States would grow into a great nation. They were not expecting the Lord to return soon. Furthermore, every Christian who understood the Scriptures that revealed the restoration of the nation of Israel before the second coming knew that Jesus could not return at any moment. Sir Isaac Newton understood this and wrote about it over 400 years ago in *Newton's Prophecies of Daniel.* So it is simply not true that the Church has always preached that Jesus is coming soon. The Church has been saying it a lot in the last few years because it is the message of the Holy Spirit... and it will soon prove to be true!

A second undeniable fact that may be related to Peter's prophecy is that there have never been so many scoffers of "the promise of His coming" as there are today. In fact, some of those very scoffers were once among those who believed that the Lord would return in the year 2000. Now they are attempting to cover their own tracks by belittling, even mocking, others who believed and taught the same thing. I have personally received a few of the most caustic and mocking letters I have ever read, telling me that I am a false prophet and a heretic—for starters. They came from people who are part of the Body of Christ.

A third fact: We can safely conclude that, in this present generation, it is highly unlikely that a "promise of His coming" will ever again be given by so many sectors of the Body of Christ regarding a specific time. Many Christian leaders are so ashamed of their pre-2000 predictions and teachings that they have openly declared they will never again touch the subject of the last days.

In the above prophecy, Peter was definitely referring to a specific time—the last days. Could it be that he was foreseeing the post-2000 period we are presently witnessing? To say that large sectors of the Church experienced a spiritual and prophetic earthquake during the time leading up to the year 2000 and afterward, when nothing happened, would be an understatement. Is it possible that Peter saw what would happen?

When the Lord did not come in the year 2000, and it seemed that nothing of great significance took place, mockers were heard on every hand. Their vitriolic scoffing has been devastating to many sincere hearts who are still looking for and longing for the Lord's coming. Their words have caused many Christians to avoid even the mention of the last days and the Lord's coming, especially the Christians who expected the Lord to return in the year 2000. Endtime subjects are now almost taboo and the faith of many has been dealt a serious blow. One of the main reasons I decided to write this book was to help those who have been shaken, as well as to present a biblical answer for some of the doubts found in many seeking hearts.

Peter's prophecy can refer to only one of two possible scenarios. One is that scoffers would arise in the last days and mock a *specific* promise of His coming that would be given in the last days (and not before then). The other is that scoffers would arise in the last days and mock a *general* promise of His coming that the Church has believed throughout the last 2,000 years. Up until recently, most of us have held to the second scenario. However, there has now been such an incredibly precise fulfillment to Peter's prophecy that maybe it's time for us to reconsider what Peter is saying.

Many presented a *specific* promise that He would come in or around the year 2000.. Now, there are many scoffers who are mocking that *specific* promise and those who made it because it was not fulfilled. One of the saddest aspects of the scenario we are witnessing is that most of the mockers are members of the Body of Christ. Peter tells us that the other apostles also warned of the coming of mockers. I doubt that Peter and the other apostles were warning us about mockers in the world. They have always existed, and really are not much of a risk. Mockers *inside* the Church are the ones who can do far greater damage to the Church than what the world can do.

Few in the Church have ever mocked the *general* promise that Jesus will return some day, and it is unlikely they ever will. All true Christians know that He will return. At this time, however, there are mockers in the Church who are mocking the *specific* promise of His coming for the year 2000 that was not fulfilled. Jude sheds light on the issue of the mockers in the last days and where they are found—in the Church! Let's consider what he says about mockers:

> *But, beloved, remember ye the words which were spoken before of the apostles of our Lord Jesus Christ; how that they told you there should be mockers in the last time, who should walk after their own ungodly lusts.* (Jude 1:17-18)

Both Peter and Jude link these mockers or scoffers (the same Greek word) in three clear ways. First, they both explain that the apostles warned they would come. Second, the apostles declared that they would come specifically in the last days. Third, both men tell us that the mockers will "walk after their own lusts." So, we can safely conclude that they are both talking about the same group of people.

Since this was part of the message of the apostles, it must be vitally important that we understand it. In fact, Peter even declares, *"Knowing this first, that there shall come in the last days scoffers..."* (II Pet. 3:3a). As he begins to deal with the issue of the last days in this passage, the first thing he wants us to know is that scoffers will come. In this present day, it seems that they have already come! However, Jude gives us an important detail that Peter also mentions, although not with as much clarity as Jude, who tells us that these people are found in the Church. Most of the short Epistle of Jude is dedicated to describing their many characteristics. Consider this summary of Jude's description of the scoffers:

> *For there are certain men crept in unawares, who were before of old ordained to this condemnation, ungodly men, turning the grace of our God into lasciviousness, and denying the only Lord God, and our Lord Jesus Christ. I will therefore put you in remembrance, though ye once knew this, how that the Lord, having saved the people out of the land of Egypt, afterward destroyed them that believed not (v. 4-5)... Woe unto them! for they have gone in the way of Cain, and ran greedily after the error of Balaam for reward, and perished in the gainsaying of Core. These are spots in your feasts of charity, when they feast with you, feeding themselves without fear: clouds they are without water, carried about of winds; trees whose fruit withereth, without fruit, twice dead, plucked up by the roots (v. 11-12)... These are murmurers, complainers, walking after*

their own lusts; and their mouth speaketh great swelling words,
having men's persons in admiration because of advantage (v. 16)...
mockers in the last time. (v. 18)

Consider Jude's salient points. These mockers have "crept into" the
Church unawares and have turned the grace of God into lasciviousness. Men of the world cannot twist the grace of God. They neither
have it nor know anything about it. Jude is saying that those who have
crept into the Church have changed the message of grace into a license
to live after the flesh. Jude then warns that although the Lord Himself
saved His people from Egypt (a symbol of the world), even so, those
who did not believe were later destroyed. They were saved by the blood of the Passover lamb (a symbol of Christ), and then they crossed the
Red Sea (a symbol of water baptism—I Cor. 10:2). Yet, later, the very
people God saved were destroyed by the One who had saved them.

Jude goes on to mention Cain, a member of the only family of God
in his day. He also mentions Balaam, a prophet who actually heard
from God but brought immorality into Israel, and Core (or Korah), a
Levite who ministered among God's people and who led a rebellion
against Moses. Jude tells us that people like these men are found in the
love feasts of the Church, feasting with the true Christians. They are
twice dead. How could that happen? Paul explains it for us, saying
that before coming to the Lord we were all dead in sin (Eph. 2:1). These
mockers were made alive by the gospel of Christ and have now died
again through the judgment of God. Why? Because they were people
who bore no fruit (Jude 12), and Jesus said that such ones would be cut
off (John 15:2, 6).

The mockers have men's persons in admiration (Jude 16). This was
one of Saul's weaknesses. He was more concerned about the opinion
and approval of man than of God. He did not want to lose the people
and therefore responded incorrectly to a delay. Is Jude telling us that
because of a desire for man's approval some will become mockers in
the last days when the promise of His coming isn't fulfilled? If so, then
their response to the delay will be to mock others so people won't reject
them by linking them to those people who went out to receive the Bridegroom and who were "foolishly" looking for His appearing.

Yes, just as it is part of God's nature to show mercy to the needy, it
is also part of God's nature to catch the wicked in their own wickedness
(Prov. 11:5). He has allowed a delay in His coming to awaken those

who "went out to meet the Bridegroom" (not physically, but in their hearts) in the year 2000. When He did not come, the needy souls reacted by humbly and gratefully realizing they were not ready for the Wedding anyway. They became thankful for a little more time to prepare themselves. It is true that the promise of His coming was not fulfilled, but that promise certainly caused many to be awakened to the lateness of the hour.

How did the proud respond to a delay? They began to mock those who had, in a spiritual sense, gone out to receive the Lord. They began to smite their fellow servants, not with their fists but with their words. Their love for the Lord and His Body grew cold. The divine delay not only revealed the lack of spiritual readiness in the hearts of the needy, it also revealed the lack of true faith and love in the hearts of the unbelieving. The hearts of these are filled with unbelief even though they are found inside the Church. Furthermore, it revealed pride in some hearts. Scoffing is a fruit that takes time to grow, and it is the fruit of an unbelieving and proud heart. A heart of faith and humility never scoffs when what it has believed is proven wrong. Rather, it seeks for understanding and light with even more diligence and humility.

Although other men may have never discerned the unbelief and pride in the hearts of the scoffers, the Lord did. When a delay came, it gave them the opportunity they needed to reveal what had always been in their hearts. Therefore, it was important for the Lord to delay His coming so that the scoffers mentioned by Peter and Jude would reveal themselves for both the Lord and others to see. What will the mocker say when the Lord comes *"on a day when he is not looking for Him and at an hour that he is not aware of"?* (Matt. 24:50). I wonder when the mockers will stop their mocking. Will it be just before He comes or just after?

Jesus did not come in the year 2000, but most of those who thought He would come in that year were people who sincerely loved Him, who loved the truth, and longed for Him to come so they could be with Him. For anyone to mock such people is surely displeasing to the Lord. It may also bring divine displeasure on them. They are scoffing at hearts that have already been crushed because they recognize that they saw through a glass darkly and didn't have the whole message. *"Whoso mocketh the poor reproacheth his Maker..."* (Prov. 17:5a). Also, *"He [God] mocks proud mockers but gives grace to the humble"* (Prov. 3:34, NIV). Once again, may the Lord give us grace to respond to a delay in a way that pleases Him.

Chapter 8

More Reasons for a Delay

Any delay in any plan almost always causes a reaction in the heart of man. Delays are one of the trials of life. Proverbs 13:12 explains what happens when we are faced with a delay: *"Hope deferred maketh the heart sick: but when the desire cometh, it is a tree of life."*

Defer, delay and postpone are synonyms. The Hebrew word "sick" also means "to become weak." A delay causes our heart to become spiritually sick or weak. When this happens, we almost always discover things in our hearts that we didn't know were there. Natural sickness does much the same. For example, certain qualities or failures in a person sometimes never come to light until that person is on a sickbed. What emerges during their suffering might be greater love and kindness than they have ever displayed, or it might be greater impatience and anger than ever.

What is inside the heart also comes out when a person grows weak. When Esau was weak from hunger, his total contempt for his birthright was revealed. He sold it to his brother, Jacob, for a bowl of pottage! That birthright included the spiritual and natural blessings of his grandfather, Abraham. Without thinking twice, he exchanged God's precious, eternal blessings for a bowl of soup because he was weak from hunger!

Uriah the Hittite also showed what was in his heart in his moment of weakness. When David was attempting to cover up his adultery with Bathsheba, the wife of Uriah, he called Uriah from the battlefield and made him drunk. He thought that in Uriah's moment of weakness he would go and spend the night with his wife in his own comfortable bed, especially after having spent weeks on the battlefield.

Then, everyone would assume that the baby in Bathsheba's womb was Uriah's. We can only imagine the blow it was to David's self-esteem when Uriah slept all night outside on the steps leading to the king's house. David discovered that morally, Uriah, at his weakest point (being drunk), was stronger than the king. What love and faithfulness Uriah revealed in his answer to David: "How can I enjoy my wife and my house when my lord, Joab, is living in the open fields?"

A tremendous, modern example of how delays or postponements expose our hearts was given by Brother Walter Buettler, one of the teachers at the Bible school where my wife attended several years before we met and got married. He was a man of impeccable character with a fervent love for the Lord. He was well known for having an ear to hear God's voice as few men alive in his day. He was also known for fearing God alone and not man.

Brother Buettler was invited to be the conference speaker at a huge gathering of many churches in a large city. When it was time for him to speak during the first night of meetings, a young pastor stood to introduce him. At one point during the introduction, the pastor declared, "Ladies and Gentlemen, tonight we have with us the great Walter Buettler." When Brother Buettler came to the pulpit, his only words were, "Soooo, we have with us the great Walter Buettler? Ladies and Gentlemen, my Father tells me that He has nothing to say to you tonight. The meeting has ended. Good night."

Many in the congregation had traveled long distances. Many had come with the hope of meeting the Lord in a fresh way. Now, their hopes had been dashed by a delay—the first message would not be given until the next night. Most of that great multitude responded in one of two ways. Many stomped out of the large auditorium, angrily asking, "Who does he think he is anyway? What right does *he* have to cancel the meeting?" As they were stomping out, others fell to their knees and began to cry out to God for forgiveness and humility. They realized that even though the flesh is very unworthy, we are often moved by self-importance, believing that there are other great ones in the earth besides the Lord.

When Brother Buettler postponed his first message, was he following the guidance of the Spirit or not? I suspect it was the greatest single message Brother Buettler ever preached! To this day, he probably is remembered more for that awesome moment than for any other. Can we be sure that the Lord was not leading Brother Buettler to do what he did? Would the Lord ever do the same sort of thing Himself? The hour had been set for the first message of the conference, but that first message was delayed a whole day.

Even though the analogy of Walter Buettler's postponement cannot compare in magnitude, could it be that the Lord established a timetable for His coming but then chose to postpone it? One thing is clear. Whether the year 2000 was an important year on the Lord's calendar or not, it certainly was thought to be an important year by many Jews and Christians. The hope that was deferred when that year passed has caused many hearts to be spiritually sick and weak. What has come out of those hearts is amazing.

The Lust In Hearts Has Been Revealed

After the year 2000 passed, many Christians who had been faithful to attend their congregations began to miss church services with more and more frequency. Others began to work harder to make more money. One man who had only small children at the time said to me, "I want to work hard so that I can leave an inheritance to my children." It was obvious that he was mocking the idea that the Lord would return soon.

Was he mocking men or was he mocking God? This is a question of great eternal importance for that man. His love of the world became evident when shortly afterward he left his church entirely. He was offended that he had been deceived into believing that the coming of the Lord was near. He told me that he had wasted valuable time, thinking that the Lord's coming was near. He said that he could have made a lot more money in business if he would have just dedicated more time to making money. To all who knew him, what he was saying was very clear. He was lamenting the fact that he had wasted so much time on his spiritual life and eternal riches during the past several years, as he sought for more of God, when he could have been accumulating more of the world's goods.

During the 30 years leading up to the year 2000, I shared the biblical and historical evidence pointing to that year as the time of Christ's return. By the year 1998 and 1999, many were sharing that Jesus would come in the year 2000 or shortly afterward. Fortunately for them, what they said was soon forgotten by those around them. After all, their ideas were relatively new to them and to those who heard them.

In the case of my ministry, I wrote a book in 1991 about the importance of the year 2000 in God's calendar; I had shared that message for so many years that, in some ways, I became identified with it. No one was going to let me forget it, and I am *very* glad they didn't! I hope we all begin to see anew that the coming of the Lord is near and that we urgently need to do whatever we must do so we'll be ready. During 40 years of ministry, our main message has been that of loving Jesus. One purpose of any endtime message should be to inspire us to love Jesus more and to love this world less so we will be ready for His appearing.

Before the year 2000, I sometimes asked congregations who had believed our message how they would react if the Lord did not come in the year 2000. I truly doubted that, if He didn't come then, any of them would react with disappointment for having dedicated too much time to their spiritual lives as a result of my teaching. I often said, "I don't think anyone is going to say, 'I wish I weren't so spiritual. I wish I had lived more for the world and less for the Lord, now that He has not come.' "

I clearly did not know the human heart and the mixture of goals, ambitions, motives and loves that reside there. In one congregation, there were a couple of young men who were in their early twenties. They both loved the Lord dearly and had been following and serving Him faithfully for many years. They had been kept from the depths of immorality and sin by the grace of God ever since they were little children. After the year 2000 passed, their mother said, "It is really too bad that we believed the message about the year 2000. If we had not believed it, my sons would have gone to the university, and they would have a degree by now."

Wait a minute! During the 30 years leading up to the year 2000, I often asked the question, "What should we do in the light of the Lord's soon coming?" My answer always was, and still is, that our response to God should be the same as it has always been—to daily seek the Lord and find out His perfect will for our lives and then do it. If going to the university is God's will for your life, then that is exactly what you should do. If He wants you to do something else, then you should do that.

Then why do we need to know that His coming is near? Because we all need to understand that we do not have 70 years to decide whether or not we are going to choose His will for our lives. His coming will definitely cut short my *own* plans for my life, but it will never cut short *His* plans for my life! He knows that I will have sufficient time to accomplish what He has called me to do. I sincerely, and naively, thought that the reaction of every Christian who believed the

Lord would come in the year 2000 would be one of thankfulness if He were to delay. Let me include here a quote from my book, *The Final Victory: The Year 2000?* This is how I thought every heart would respond:

> And if His coming is delayed or our understanding is in error, they will continue to be thankful for every additional day that they, as well as others, are being granted to know the King in still deeper ways (p. 347).

The mother of those young men was either saying that she and her family did not seek God's will for their lives, or that now she wished they had not obeyed God's will. Clearly, other goals and motives were in her heart long before the year 2000. The delay simply caused them to surface. Oh yes, she wanted to be ready for the coming of the Lord. After all, who wants to miss that blessing? But she was not all that concerned about doing His will, at least not if there was still time for her to do her own will.

In her heart, if the Lord wasn't going to come soon, there were other goals more important to her than doing God's will. She, her husband and her boys had all believed previously that it was not God's will for the boys to attend the university and risk being destroyed by the influences of the world. This is what happens to many young people who go to college. Suddenly, after the year 2000, what they had openly confessed for years to be God's will no longer mattered. They began to smite those around them, not with their hands but with their words. They criticized both the leadership of the church and its members, and finally stopped attending the church.

Let me be quick to explain that, over the years, many of the young people associated with our ministry have attended universities. Many are still studying and others have already graduated. I firmly believe that if higher education is God's will for a young person, then God will protect their spiritual lives during their time of study. If the Lord returns while they are studying, there is nothing better they could be doing at the time of His coming than the perfect will of God. However, anyone who chooses a path outside of God's will runs the risk of serious consequences.

The issue with the father of the little children and the mother of the young men mentioned previously was the condition of their hearts, which might never have been revealed if there had not been a delay. Jesus said:

But and if that evil servant shall say in his heart, My lord delayeth his coming; and shall begin to smite his fellowservants, and to eat and drink with the drunken; the lord of that servant shall... appoint him his portion with the hypocrites: there shall be weeping and gnashing of teeth. (Matt. 24:48-51)

The problem in the life of this evil servant began in his heart. In fact, the Lord would only call a person "evil" if his heart is evil. Israel in the wilderness erred "in their heart" (Heb. 3:10) and they had an "evil heart of unbelief" (Heb. 3:12). Why did the father of the little children begin to live for the flesh and this present world? Because the lust of other things was already in his heart and the delay merely revealed it. He did not mock because the Lord did not return. He mocked because of the unbelief that had been in his heart for years... the delay caused it to surface. He also mocked because of his own ungodly lusts as Jude said would happen.

The mother of the young men did not begin to smite others with the sword of her mouth (her words), because of a delay. Rather, the delay revealed what had been in her heart for many years—a love of this world and the things of the world. It is true she was disappointed that the Lord did not return. If He had only returned at the time she thought He would return, her lack of spiritual oil would never have been revealed! But her hope had been deferred and it made her heart sick and weak. Then what was in her heart began to come out.

It is noteworthy that the Lord appoints the wicked servant a place with the hypocrites. Hypocrites are people who speak one thing outwardly but who are different on the inside. This is precisely what a delay revealed in the life of the wicked servant. It is precisely what the delay we have just experienced has revealed in the lives of a good number of Christians. Some of them did not even know what was in their hearts. The Lord tells us that *"the heart is deceitful above all things, and desperately wicked: who can know it?"* (Jer. 17:9). Of course, I am not referring to people that were new believers just prior to the year 2000. Many of them were simply caught up in the moment and their hearts were pure in this regard.

A Delay Gives Time for Repentance

None of us really know our own hearts. The father and mother of those young men did not know theirs. When the Lord allows what is in our hearts to be revealed, it is not primarily to enable those around us to see how terrible we are. Rather, it is so we ourselves can see what we are and repent... while there is still hope of being changed. The Lord does not want anyone to perish. He is merciful and forgiving. He is willing to forgive and restore all who humble themselves before Him. Peter reveals the Lord's desire for each one of us:

The Lord is not slow in keeping his promise, as some understand slowness. He is patient with you, not wanting anyone to perish, but everyone to come to repentance. (II Pet. 3:9, NIV)

Peter makes this declaration in the context of the mockers in the last days who walk after their own lusts. What a God! What hope! What mercy! They mock at the seemingly failed promise of His coming because there is lust in their hearts that they didn't even know was there, and then He holds out mercy to them. He knows we are but dust (Psa. 103:14). He knows that we are prone to fall and to fail. Yet, He is a patient, loving, kind and merciful heavenly Father.

Few men in history could have understood what Peter was writing here to the degree that Peter himself understood it. He was the disciple who recognized the Lord. While others thought that Jesus might be Elijah or some other prophet, Peter knew that they were walking with the Christ, the King of glory. He was determined to follow his God to the end. During the last supper, Peter had difficulty convincing Jesus that he was more determined to follow Him than any of the other disciples. But Jesus also had difficulty—convincing Peter that he did not know what was in his own heart and that before the cock would crow twice, Peter would deny Him three times.

Peter was certain that the Lord simply did not know him well enough to make a proper evaluation. He was certain, that is, until he began "to curse and to swear, saying, I know not the man" and the cock crowed the second time (Mk. 14:72). Then, Peter went out and wept bitterly. He must have wept from great sorrow as he saw his own condition and realized how pride and ambition had blinded him. He most certainly wept even more as he meditated on the glory he had witnessed in the Lord and that, in spite of that glory, he had denied knowing Him. To have been sure that He was the Messiah and then to have denied Him was more than any human heart could have endured. However, his greatest sorrow must have been the solemn realization that he would never see the Lord nor find His favor again. What man would not arrive at this conclusion upon finding himself in such a state of despair and failure?

Peter did not really know the Lord, yet he thought the Lord was the One who did not know him and the depth of his commitment. Peter soon discovered that he did not know himself nor the depths of wickedness in his own heart. But we will see in a moment that he was also soon to discover the depths of God's mercy! As he wept, he certainly thought that he had forever lost his place in the Kingdom of God. He was sure that his Lord would never even want to see him again.

It doesn't require a lot of imagination to visualize what happened when the disciples heard the initial reports that the Lord had risen. The risen Lord Himself had told the women to go and tell the disciples to travel to Galilee to meet with Him there (Matt. 28:10). Imagine what the scene might have been like at that moment. Upon hearing the Lord's command, they all would have arisen immediately to depart for Galilee. But Peter would have remained in his place, still weeping, as they all went out the door. They would have said to him, "Come on, Peter. The Lord wants us to be with Him in Galilee." Peter would almost certainly have responded, "No! I am sure He never wants to see me again. You fellows go ahead. I'm afraid my life has come to an end. I denied Him in His hour of need. How could He not deny me now? I am sure that He was not inviting me."

Yes, all of this scenario would have happened except for one thing. After the Lord had departed from the women who had arrived at the tomb early that resurrection morning, some of them apparently stayed behind. Upon entering the tomb they encountered an angel who gave them much the same instructions that Jesus had given them, but he added two small words, obviously in obedience to the Lord's own instructions. He said, *"But go your way, tell his disciples and Peter that he goeth before you into Galilee: there shall ye see him, as he said unto you"* (Mark 16:7).

Imagine the above scene once again now that Peter has specifically been invited! Just as Peter would have been telling his fellow disciples that he was sure that he had not been invited, someone said, "But, Peter, the angel clearly said that the Lord wants to see all of His disciples *and Peter* in Galilee! That can only mean He still loves and accepts you, Peter!" The Lord Himself knew that Peter would have never accompanied the other disciples to see Him without calling him by name. What a merciful God we serve! He added those little words, "And Peter," surely transforming Peter's tears into joy. Of all men, Peter knew what he was writing about in II Peter 3:9. He had learned by experience that the weakest souls, and even those who mock the Lord's promises, are invited to find their place at the feet of the Lord once again.

Maybe we too have failed Him in these last days. Maybe we have even mocked the promise of His coming because of other desires and loves in our own hearts. The God of Peter is still alive, and He is our God. He is the God of forgiveness and restoration. He will not reject us if we do not continue to reject Him. His arms are open to every repentant soul, inviting us to return to Him. We should all rejoice if we are experiencing a divine delay. The delay has revealed what is in many hearts, and it gives us time to repent and have our hearts cleansed from the things that might have caused us to mock. Because of the Lord's mercy, even if you have also gravely failed Him like Peter did, you can put your own name in place of Peter's name in the Lord's invitation to His disciples *and Peter*. He does not only call His other disciples to be with Him. He also calls *you* to be with Him!

Chapter 9

Everyone Needed a Delay

If there has been a delay in the Lord's coming, we can rest assured that it was the best plan for every believer alive today. In God's Kingdom, whatever is in the best interest of one individual is always in the best interest of everyone. God never needs to jeopardize one person in order to bless another. Most of us needed more time to prepare for His coming. Also, the Lord wanted to give the scoffers time to reveal what was in their hearts, and then time to repent. But there are two other very important purposes for a delay.

Pride Has Been Avoided

The Apostle Paul needed a thorn in his flesh to keep him humble because of his revelations (II Cor. 12:7). How much more do we all need divine help to remain humble any time the Lord shares His secrets with us. Many people, including me, believed the Lord had given us understanding of His divine calendar. Based on that understanding, we expected the Lord to return in the year 2000. Of course, we also knew that certain prophetic events had to occur during the years immediately before the year 2000.

I can well imagine what might have happened in our hearts if, prior to the year 2000, the prophetic events associated with the Lord's coming would have been fulfilled. Once it became apparent that our message was going to be fulfilled on time, it is almost a certainty that every one of us would have gone to great lengths to get the message out. The message we would have tried to get out would not necessarily have been the message of the Lord's coming and our urgent need to prepare. Rather, there would have been an enormous temptation to ensure that the whole world knew we were the favored ones to whom the Lord had revealed the time of His coming. Maybe others would have even considered us to be among the prophets who hear the voice of the Spirit with precision! Of course, the Lord is able to keep anyone humble regardless of how great he or she becomes in the Kingdom of God, but I still wonder whether or not pride would have overcome us.

Since the days of Paul, few, if any, have reached his level of spirituality. Yet, the Lord was able to maintain humility in the heart of one so great as Paul through a thorn in his flesh. The Lord has succeeded in either maintaining or else creating humility in those who thought they knew the time of His coming. It seems that He has accomplished this with a delay rather than with a thorn.

I continue to honestly believe that all the evidence regarding the year 2000 presented by sincere Christians and Jews was not totally wrong. I believe the problem was that we saw (and still see) through a glass darkly, and we did not see that the Lord had forewarned us about a delay. Yet, today more than ever, it seems unlikely that anyone would have a problem with pride resulting from an understanding of the Lord's calendar. After all, those of us who thought we understood the Lord's calendar have received help to humble ourselves from many sources. With mockers on every side, and with letters of condemnation coming in from time to time, how could anyone be proud about knowing something that has brought such reproach? It has been a crushing experience for those of us who taught about this theme, not just for those who heard and believed our message.

Whether we were right or wrong about the calendar, and whether we are now in a time of delay or not, one thing is certain—there is more humility in many hearts than there was before. Unfortunately, some have reacted incorrectly to the humiliation, determined that they will avoid further humiliation by never making such a mistake again. To do so, they plan on eliminating all or most of the endtime teaching from their ministries. Others, however, are still willing to risk their reputations and risk being humbled again as they diligently search for the truth. Surely this reaction is more pleasing to the Lord. Lovers of truth who react this way will see that they have received a double blessing from the delay. They have received more humility, and they will now be more cautious than they ever were in how they handle the Word of God. But they will never purposely avoid any theme found in His Word, not even themes about the last days.

There Is Still Time to Buy Oil

When the ten virgins realized that the bridegroom was delaying His coming, they slumbered and slept. It was not the best thing for any of them to do. The wise virgins had enough oil to reach the time of His coming, but did they have enough joy? The long-awaited wedding was at hand. This wedding was not just another wedding. This story and this wedding were symbolic of the Wedding of the Creator with His eternal Bride, the Church.

Though the wise virgins were sleeping instead of seeking Him, at least they were ready for the wedding. But the sleep of the foolish virgins spelled tragedy. For them, the bridegroom's delay in coming did two things. First, the delay revealed their need for more oil. Second, the delay gave them time to pay the price to obtain the oil. We have already seen how merciful the Lord is to the mockers. His delay revealed their mocking hearts, and the delay gives them time to repent and be saved. He reveals His mercy to the foolish virgins in much the same way. The Lord has always dealt with man this way. He not only shows us our need, but He shows us the answer to our need. He never leaves us without hope.

How will we react to the delay? Will we enter into spiritual sleep and discouragement or will we seek Him and rejoice? Will we slumber and sleep or will we arise and buy more oil? Will we mock or will we humble our hearts and seek understanding? Will we scoff or will we repent? Will we take the understanding of the Lord's calendar that many in the Church and among the Jews seem to have received and categorize it all as nothing more than the concoction of men? Will we refuse to study the last days ever again and avoid teaching on this subject? Will we begin to smite others with our words and choose to live for the flesh and the world? Or, will we repent of the mistakes we have made as a result of seeing through a glass darkly and continue to humbly seek for understanding of the times just as the prophets of old did?

Yes, a delay has caused a different reaction in each believer, and that delay seems to have been an essential part of God's plan from the beginning... because every believer needed a delay. In fact, it appears that a delay is just one more example of the Lord's great wisdom in dealing with man.

Chapter 10

Indications That the Delay Will Be Short

If the delay in the Lord's coming proves to be short, will we rejoice or weep? Much will depend on our reaction to the delay and how we use our time during the delay. If we use our time wisely to seek the Lord, and receive grace to obey Him, we will rejoice when He comes. Unfortunately, some will weep. They will not only weep because they are not ready, but because they foolishly thought the delay would be longer, or maybe they didn't believe that the Lord's coming was even near. After the year 2000, the attitude of some Christians was revealed by their declaration—"Who knows? The Lord might not return for another thousand years. Let's not be overly concerned with His coming."

There is a solid biblical basis for declaring that the delay will be short. This is even more evident when one compares biblical prophecies with world events at this time. The Lord's parable of the ten virgins gives us at least an indication that the delay will be short. The ten virgins went out to receive the bridegroom, thinking they knew approximately when He would come, and they all had enough oil to last until that time. But then He delayed.

If the Lord had wanted to give the idea that the bridegroom's delay would be prolonged, then the virgins in His parable would have gone back home instead of waiting outside. In the parable, the delay was clearly very short. Maybe they thought that He would come at nine o'clock in the evening, and in the parable it turned out that He came at midnight. So, it was not a long delay. The bridegroom came during the same night that they went out to wait for him; in the parable the delay was short. If this is not part of the message of the parable, then the problem is that the parable gives us a detail that the Lord expects us to ignore.

For many years I believed and taught an idea that is sometimes promoted regarding the parables and symbols found in the Bible, stating that parables and symbols are only shadows and as such, are not precise, but only approximately correct. This idea proves to be faulty in light of the Bible and science.

A shadow is cast when a person or object is exposed to light. If we look at the shadow of any object or person, it is not complete, but it is totally reliable and exact. For example, if the body of a person is casting the shadow, then we will never find anything in the shadow that is not found on the person. If the shadow has a head, two arms and two legs, we will definitely be able to find them on the person. It is true that the shadow does not show every detail about the person, yet nothing found in the shadow is incorrect. Although the angle of the light can cause a shadow to be long or short, the light can neither add nor subtract details, and neither should we when we study biblical shadows.

Paul tells us that the person who cast the shadow across the Bible, giving us symbols or shadows, was Christ Himself (Col. 2:16-17). Therefore, the symbols or shadows in the Bible, as well as all of the Lord's parables, are correct and trustworthy. They never present a complete picture, but neither do they ever present an incorrect picture. Because of this, I now teach that if my doctrine does not fit a biblical parable, it is proof that I need to change my doctrine, not the parable! Once I have the truth, I will never need to ignore part of the message of a parable and pretend it is not there. Surely, the fact that the bridegroom came during the same night that the virgins went out to meet him is significant and indicates a short delay in his coming.

Let's consider a Bible story that might indicate that His coming is nearer than many believe.

Goliath and the Son of David

We considered briefly why it is significant that Christ has inherited the throne of His father David (Lk. 1:32). At a minimum, this tells us that David's throne was an Old Testament prophetic revelation of what Christ's throne would be like in the New Testament. Of course, the man who sat on that throne is the key message. David was a man after God's own heart. He was Christ-like. The Psalms show us just how prophetic the very life and experiences of David were. This is demonstrated by the many times that the Psalms are quoted in the New Testament and applied to Christ's own life and experiences (e.g., Jn. 13:18 and Psa. 41:9). The Psalms are quoted in the New Testament more than any other Old Testament book.

Although David was such a skilled worshiper that he was chosen to play the harp before King Saul, it wasn't that aspect of his life that caused him to be well known in Israel. King Saul himself did not take enough interest in his young court musician to even know who David's father was (I Sam. 17:56). What catapulted David into national fame and became his first major step toward ascending to the throne of Israel was his victory over the giant Goliath.

Afterward, the women came out to meet both David and Saul. They sang, *"Saul hath slain his thousands, and David his ten thousands"* (I Sam. 18:7). Immediately, Saul saw the handwriting on the wall and was very angry. He responded, *"They have ascribed unto David ten thousands, and to me they have ascribed but thousands: and what can he have more but the kingdom?"* (I Sam. 18:8).

The story of David and Goliath makes a wonderful lesson for children. But I doubt that David thought of his battle with Goliath as a good Sunday school story when he was staring into the face of a heavily armed and well-trained nine-and-a-half-foot man! Maybe we have minimized, to some degree, the prophetic importance of this moment in David's life. It is difficult to find anything recorded in Scripture about the life of David that is not prophetic. But his victory over Goliath was one of the most amazing moments of his life. How could it not be prophetic?

Killing Goliath was one of the pivotal moments in David's life. It was his first major battle and victory on behalf of all Israel. What, then, could be its prophetic fulfillment in the life of the Son of David? It must be related in some way to an initial battle that the Lord wins for all Israel as He ascends to the throne. Could this have some endtime fulfillment? Let's consider both the events that led up to David's battle with Goliath and the battle itself.

History seems to be repeating itself in our day, and maybe we have not noticed.

During the years before David came to the throne, Israel experienced continual battles with the Philistines. Actually, the word Palestinians in the Hebrew has been translated as "Philistines" in most

English versions of the Bible. In other words, "Palestinians" comes directly from Hebrew. Whom has Israel been in continual battles with throughout its modern history? With the Palestinians—with the Philistines once again! Let's call them by their Hebrew name, "Palestinians" to help us make the connection.

During the course of Israel's long war with the Palestinians in the time of David, a Palestinian giant appeared on the scene, defying the armies of Israel for 40 days (I Sam. 17:16). In some passages of the Bible, 40 days represent 40 years. Ezekiel was commanded to lie on one side during 40 days to represent 40 years. The Lord told him, *"I have appointed thee each day for a year"* (Ezek. 4:6). Of course, in the mind of almost any Jewish person the number 40 is forever associated with the 40 years that Israel wandered in the wilderness.

The New Testament also associates 40 days with the 40-year wilderness journey. The Lord told Israel that one of the main purposes of that journey was to teach them *"that man doth not live by bread only, but by every word that proceedeth out of the mouth of the LORD doth man live"* (Deut. 8:2-3).

It is no coincidence that Jesus spent 40 days in that same wilderness, and then, at the end of those days, He was tempted by Satan to turn stones into bread. He responded by declaring to Satan the main lesson that Israel was supposed to learn during their 40 years in the wilderness. He said, *"It is written, Man shall not live by bread alone, but by every word that proceedeth out of the mouth of God"* (Matt. 4:4). The Son of God had learned in 40 days what Israel had difficulty learning during 40 years.

If the story of David and Goliath contains a prophetic message regarding the last days, then it could be that a Palestinian will arise and defy the armies of Israel during 40 years. The world recognizes today that the best known political leader on earth, barring none, is Yasser Arafat, the Palestinian giant. (I give documentation for this statement in my book, *Yasser Arafat—An Apocalyptic Character?*)

Is it sheer coincidence that Yasser Arafat founded his Fatah terrorist organization in the 1960s, and that we are coming to the end of a period of 40 years in which he has successfully defied the armies of Israel? Is it sheer coincidence that, for literally decades, news media articles have frequently likened the battle between Israel and Arafat to David and Goliath? Since the world is under the control of Satan, the "god of this world," it is understandable that they would do a 180-degree twist on the truth. They liken Israel to Goliath and Arafat to David, but the fact remains—Satan's kingdom sees a prophetic connection between this Palestinian and the story of Goliath, the Palestinian.

As in the case of Goliath, people's attention is drawn immediately to Arafat's physical stature, ironically, for the opposite reason it was drawn to Goliath's. He is one of the shortest leaders in history, standing 5 feet 4 inches. However, his physical stature belies his spiritual stature. There is little doubt that Satan himself is behind the power that Arafat has wielded for so many years. He has successfully defied the armies of the third strongest military power on earth. Israel's intelligence community and covert operations expertise are second to none. In spite of this, over the course of many years, Israel has failed repeatedly in their attempts to assassinate Yasser Arafat; he has miraculously survived every time. Of course, now they are actually doing everything they can to avoid killing him because world opinion is on Arafat's side.

It may be that the Son of David will be the only One who will succeed in ending the threats and defiance of this spiritual giant. He continues to strike terror into the hearts of Israel just as Goliath did. He kills the Jewish people at will and the world blames Israel if they take any serious measures to stop him. He is allowed to blow up buses filled with children, but Israel is not allowed to accidentally kill even one civilian in their attempts to stop Arafat and his terrorists.

Maybe the first battle and victory that the Lord will obtain for Israel, as He ascends to the throne, will be with this Philistine. Is the Lord giving us a message through all the similarities between Israel's extended war with the Palestinians before David took the throne and their present, long war with the Palestinians before the Son of David takes the throne? If He is, then these details are not merely sheer coincidence and the delay in His coming will be short. Arafat doesn't have much longer to live. In April of 2003 he will reach 74 years of age. The Son of David is able to put an end to his life, either by natural or supernatural means. But if He does so, and brings an end to the power of the Palestinians, then surely the Lord's return and His coming Kingdom are near at hand.

In future chapters we will see several more reasons why we can be confident that the delay will be short. Of course, what the Lord considers a "short" time can seem like a long time to us. For Him, a short delay might be twenty years. However, we will consider further evidence that seems to indicate His delay will not be that long.

Chapter 11

The Sign of the Resurrection and Rapture

Over and over, the Bible gives us an unmistakable sign to indicate when the resurrection and rapture are at hand. I am not referring to knowing the day or the hour of those events, but to knowing the "times and seasons" (as God's Word tells us we should know). In this chapter, we will consider the sign for the time of the resurrection that Jesus, Paul, and the prophets give us. In the next chapter, we will see the same sign revealed in the Book of Revelation. It is clear that the delay will be short.

Paul Reveals the Sign of the Resurrection

Paul gives the promise of a resurrection and rapture in I Thessalonians 4:16-18, and then continues on speaking about when and how they will occur. His very next statement is as follows in I Thessalonians 5:1-5:

1 But of the times and the seasons, brethren, ye have no need that I write unto you.

2 For yourselves know perfectly that the day of the Lord so cometh as a thief in the night.

3 For when they shall say, Peace and safety; then sudden destruction cometh upon them, as travail upon a woman with child; and they shall not escape.

4 But ye, brethren, are not in darkness, that that day should overtake you as a thief.

5 Ye are all the children of light, and the children of the day: we are not of the night, nor of darkness.

Paul begins this passage with the word "but," thus connecting these statements with what he had just explained about the resurrection and rapture. He assumes that the Thessalonians understand the times and seasons associated with those events. He then seems to make contradictory statements. In verse 2, he writes that the Lord will come as a thief in the night. Then, in verses 4 and 5, he explains that the Lord cannot come to His own people as a thief in the night because they do not live in the night. In other words, He comes to the world as a thief in the night, but not to the Church. The Church should have understanding of the times and seasons.

Between these seemingly contradictory statements, Paul gives us the key to knowing the times and seasons. He writes in verse 3:

> *For when they shall say, Peace and safety; then sudden destruction cometh upon them, as travail upon a woman with child; and they shall not escape.*

In the time of the end, someone will say, "Peace and safety." Also, in the time of the end, someone will experience travail as a woman with child. If we can determine who will face this travail in the end, then we will also know who will say, "Peace and safety."

The prophet Jeremiah provides the answer. In Jeremiah 30, he leaves no doubt as to what time in history his vision in that chapter refers. At the end of his message there, he explains, *"In the latter days you will understand this"* (Jer. 30:24b, NAS). So the message of Jeremiah 30 is for the last days, and he tells us precisely who will face travail as a woman with child in the last days:

> *Ask ye now, and see whether a man doth travail with child? Wherefore do I see every man with his hands on his loins, as a woman in travail, and all faces are turned into paleness? Alas! for that day is great, so that none is like it: it is even the time of Jacob's trouble; but he shall be saved out of it.* (Jer. 30:6-7)

It is Jacob who will travail as a woman. Later, in Jeremiah 30:10, he tells us that Jacob is Israel. So then, it is also Israel who will say "Peace and safety" in the last days. Amazingly, during the last 10 years, every political campaign in every election in Israel has been based on which Prime Minister will bring peace and safety to Israel. Almost every day, the front page of *The Jerusalem Post* either has an article on how the peace process is progressing (or failing) or on the latest terrorist attack.

Is Israel in travail today? If we compare the death of almost 3,000 people in the attack on the World Trade Center with what is happening in Israel, the horrendous travail that Israel has faced for several decades comes into focus. When the United States, a nation of 280 million, loses 3,000 people, it has the equivalent impact on the nation as when Israel loses 54 people, since Israel is a nation of only 5 million. Often, many more than 54 people are either killed or maimed for life in a single terrorist attack in Israel, and at least some level of attack occurs there almost hourly.

However, the tragic end of Paul's declaration is that "sudden destruction" will come upon the nation of Israel and "they shall not escape." Something else that is tragic is that few Christians or Jews believe that the present nation of Israel will be conquered. Unfortunately, this mistaken belief is not founded on Scripture, and tragically, it will shake the faith of many who will be asking, "Where is God?"

In this chapter and the next we will present a number of Scriptures showing that the Lord will come precisely for the purpose of rescuing the remnant of His people who survive the sudden destruction in the last days. We will discover that the Lord will return *after* Israel, as a nation, is destroyed. In I Thessalonians 5:1-5, Paul is showing us that the Church's knowledge of this fact is one reason the Lord will not come to us by surprise as a thief in the night. When we see Israel's destruction, we will know that His coming is at hand. After He comes, He will then gather His people back to Israel, and they will live in peace forever under His rule.

Is sudden destruction near at hand for Israel? On December 10, 1996, the Task Force on Terrorism and Unconventional Warfare from the House of Representatives in the United States made public an eleven-page report. The report stated that seven Islamic nations were planning to attack Israel soon with nuclear, biological and chemical bombs. The report expected an attack in a matter of weeks. By the end of 2003, seven years will have passed since that report predicted the soon destruction of Israel. The Lord has had great mercy on His people!

The report explained the logic guiding these Islamic nations. They see themselves as being big enough to survive any nuclear retaliation Israel is capable of launching against them, but they believe Israel cannot survive what Islam is capable of doing to Israel. Israel's sudden destruction is at hand. Therefore, the Lord's delay will be short.

Zechariah Reveals the Sign of the Resurrection

Zechariah's prophecy of the return of the Lord needs absolutely no interpretation once we understand that the fall of the nation of Israel is what will bring about the coming of the Lord. Zechariah 14:1-4 says:

1 Behold, the day of the LORD cometh, and thy spoil shall be divided in the midst of thee.

2 For I will gather all nations against Jerusalem to battle; and the city shall be taken, and the houses rifled, and the women ravished; and half of the city shall go forth into captivity, and the residue of the people shall not be cut off from the city.

3 Then shall the LORD go forth, and fight against those nations, as when he fought in the day of battle.

4 And his feet shall stand in that day upon the mount of Olives, which is before Jerusalem on the east, and the mount of Olives shall cleave in the midst thereof toward the east and toward the west, and there shall be a very great valley; and half of the mountain shall remove toward the north, and half of it toward the south.

Paul did not see a need to write to the Thessalonians about the times and seasons related to the "day of the Lord." If they were familiar with this passage, we can understand why. It begins by saying that "the day of the Lord" is at hand. Obviously, it will be at hand when the events in this passage are fulfilled. It goes on to show us that just before the Lord descends on the Mount of Olives, the city of Jerusalem is taken and many Jews flee into captivity ("captivity" is a biblical concept that refers to Israel being scattered among the nations). Normally, when the capital city of a nation has been conquered, that nation has fallen and its government has ceased to exist. The rest of Zechariah 14 establishes beyond doubt that the Lord's descent on the Mount of Olives is the second coming, when He will establish His worldwide Kingdom upon the earth.

Most evangelical theologians believe the Bible teaches us that the second coming of the Lord will not occur until Israel repents. Unfortunately, Israel will not repent until they are crushed. In a moment, we will see that Daniel makes this clear, declaring that Israel will be totally crushed at the end of a period of three and a half years during which the nation will experience the worst time of anguish in its history. Then the resurrection will occur because it is not until then that Israel will repent and be restored to her God. However, Paul teaches us in Romans 11:15 that when Israel is restored, the resurrection will occur. Clearly, the resurrection cannot occur until Israel is crushed: *"For if the casting away of them [Israel] be the reconciling of the world, what shall the receiving of them be, but life from the dead?"* (Rom. 11:15)

The resurrection will occur when Israel is reconciled to the Lord. Zechariah, Daniel and others reveal that this reconciliation will take place at the very end, just before the Lord's second coming. Therefore, the resurrection cannot occur seven years before the end and Israel's restoration, as is sometimes taught. The resurrection will occur just *after* Israel is destroyed and just *before* the second coming, because when Israel is destroyed they will be reconciled. If we understand this, it is then easy to see why Paul links the time of the resurrection with the destruction of Israel. He obviously was familiar with the message of Zechariah 14—that the Lord will come when Israel is destroyed because it will only be then that they will be reconciled to the Lord; when they are reconciled, the resurrection will occur.

(Note: Some students of Bible prophecy believe that the resurrection, rapture and second coming all occur at the same time. This belief does not affect the message of this book, yet I do believe there will be a catching up to heavenly places first that will take the Bride of Christ to the Marriage. Shortly afterward, the heavens are opened and the Lord and His saints descend to the earth and the battle of Armageddon begins. This is the scenario presented in Revelation 19:7-15.)

Maybe the battle against Jerusalem has already begun. On September 28, 2000, Yasser Arafat, backed by the Islamic world, declared war against Israel. He has declared that his goal is to take control of Jerusalem and make it the capital of a Palestinian nation in the Holy Land. Six of the seven nations that the Task Force on Terrorism and Unconventional Warfare declared were allied for the purpose of destroying Israel appear in Psalm 83:4-8. There, they have biblical names, but their goal is the same as Islam's goal at this moment—*"Come, and let us cut them off from being a nation, that the name of Israel may be remembered no more"* (v. 4). The delay will be short.

Daniel Reveals the Sign of the Resurrection

Consider what Daniel 12:1-7 (NKJV) reveals:

1 At that time Michael shall stand up, the great prince who stands watch over the sons of your people; and there shall be a time of trouble, such as never was since there was a nation, even to that time. And at that time your people shall be delivered, every one who is found written in the book.

2 And many of those who sleep in the dust of the earth shall awake, some to everlasting life, some to shame and everlasting contempt.

3 Those who are wise shall shine like the brightness of the firmament, and those who turn many to righteousness like the stars forever and ever.

4 But you, Daniel, shut up the words, and seal the book until the time of the end; many shall run to and fro, and knowledge shall increase.

5 Then I, Daniel, looked; and there stood two others, one on this riverbank and the other on that riverbank.

6 And one said to the man clothed in linen, who was above the waters of the river, How long shall the fulfillment of these wonders be?

7 Then I heard the man clothed in linen, who was above the waters of the river, when he held up his right hand and his left hand to heaven, and swore by Him who lives forever, that it shall be for a time, times, and half a time; and when the power of the holy people has been completely shattered, all these things shall be finished.

As with Zechariah 14, this passage needs no interpretation; it is actually part of God's own interpretation of Daniel's visions. In verse 6, someone asks how long it will be until "these wonders" are fulfilled. Regardless of what else this passage reveals, it definitely reveals at least two very great wonders. The first wonder is found in verse 1. It is the greatest time of trouble since there was a nation. The second wonder is the resurrection from the dead found in verse 2.

In verse 7, we are given the key to knowing when these two events will be fulfilled. This time of trouble will be "*for a time, times, and half a time.*" By comparing Revelation 12:6 and 14, we learn that this phrase refers to a period of three and a half years. But the final phrase of verse 7 is the key thought: "*When the power of the holy people has been completely shattered, all these things shall be finished.*"

All the wonders found in Daniel 12 will be fulfilled when Israel is completely crushed. This includes the second wonder—the resurrection.

How can we be sure that "Daniel's people" in Daniel 12:1 and the "holy people" in Daniel 12:7 both refer to Israel? The Book of Daniel answers that question for us. In Daniel 9, Daniel's people are those who came out of Egypt (v. 15); they were judged and taken to Babylon for their sin (v. 1-2, 5-7); and their name is Israel (v. 20). In Daniel 10:14, the angel from heaven told Daniel, *"Now I am come to make thee understand what shall befall thy people in the latter days... "* He then gives Daniel the revelation found in Daniel 11-12. In Daniel 12:1, the conflict comes upon Daniel's people, Israel, and this same people continue to be the theme in Daniel 12:7.

Daniel gives us the same sign for knowing the time of the resurrection that Paul and Zechariah give us—the "sudden destruction" of Israel from which they will not escape. May we intercede before the Lord so that many of the Jewish people will survive... that there will be a remnant saved by His mercy. Paul declares that "all Israel will be saved" in Romans 11:26, but prior to that, in Romans 9:27, he tells us that "all Israel" will only be a "remnant." The world stage is set for the soon destruction of Israel. The delay will be short.

Jesus Reveals the Sign of the Resurrection

Consider the Lord's endtime teaching in Luke 21:20-24:

20 And when ye shall see Jerusalem compassed with armies, then know that the desolation thereof is nigh.

21 Then let them which are in Judaea flee to the mountains; and let them which are in the midst of it depart out; and let not them that are in the countries enter thereinto.

22 For these be the days of vengeance, that all things which are written may be fulfilled.

23 But woe unto them that are with child, and to them that give suck, in those days! For there shall be great distress in the land, and wrath upon this people.

24 And they shall fall by the edge of the sword, and shall be led away captive into all nations: and Jerusalem shall be trodden down of the Gentiles, until the times of the Gentiles be fulfilled.

Some believe that this passage was fulfilled in the time of the destruction of Jerusalem by Titus, the Roman general. However, the Lord's words here refer to events that will occur in the last days. The evidence found within this passage is too convincing to believe otherwise. In verse 22, Jesus tells us that He is referring to days in which *"all things that are written"* will be fulfilled. There are many written prophecies that have not yet been fulfilled, including the promise of His coming. We need go no further than Luke 19:44 to see something that is written that has never been fulfilled, definitely not in Titus' day.

As Jesus wept over the city of Jerusalem (Lk. 19:41), He declared that *"they shall not leave in thee one stone upon another"* (Lk. 19:44b). Titus did not fulfill this. My wife and I have visited the Western Wall in Jerusalem many times. On a number of occasions, we have walked through the tunnel at the base of the wall that runs almost its whole length. That wall is over 1,500 feet long and about 60 feet high. It is made of enormous stones, some over ten feet long, three feet thick and two feet tall, each one weighing many tons. Those stones were there when Jesus declared that not one stone in the city of Jerusalem would remain upon another, and neither Titus nor anyone else has ever moved them. Since Jesus is giving us details about a time when "all things which are written" will be fulfilled, we know that He is referring to the last days.

Some claim that the Lord's prophecy about the stones of Jerusalem refers only to spiritual stones or Christians. A principle of God's Word is that people, things and events in the natural world can be symbolic of, or shadows of the spiritual world (Rom. 1:20; Heb. 8:1-5). The Bible also teaches us that the corresponding event in the natural realm occurs *before* its spiritual counterpart is fulfilled. For example, there was a natural man on earth before there was a spiritual man on earth (I Cor. 15:45-46). It is, at a minimum, risky to spiritualize a biblical prophecy and then assume that its natural and literal fulfillment will never occur.

When the Lord declares, *"There shall be great distress in the land, and wrath upon this people"* (v. 23b), we are reminded of Daniel's prophecy about the worst time of anguish in history for Daniel's people, Israel. Jesus is speaking here about Jerusalem, the same people. So this wrath comes upon the people of Israel. Jesus goes on to explain, *"They shall fall by the edge of the sword"* (v. 24a). In other words, war comes to Jerusalem. In Zechariah 14:2-4, war comes to Jerusalem just before the second coming of Christ. Jesus goes on to say that they *"shall be led away captive into all nations"* (v. 24b). This further confirms the revelation of Zechariah 14:2(b)—*"half of the city shall go forth into captivity."*

"And Jerusalem shall be trodden down of the Gentiles, until the times of the Gentiles be fulfilled" (v. 24c). In the Greek, the phrase "trodden down" (from "to tread down") refers to having something under one's

feet or under one's dominion. In Psalm 8:6 and Hebrews 2:8 we are told that the Lord put all things under man's feet, giving him dominion over them. Joshua understood this symbolism when he commanded the captains of Israel's army to put their feet upon the necks of the conquered kings of Canaan (Josh. 10:24) to demonstrate dominion over them.

According to Revelation 11:2, Jerusalem will definitely be under the dominion of the Gentiles during the last three and a half years. This fact provides further evidence that in Luke 21:24 the Lord is speaking about the very last days, because there He tells us that once Jerusalem is under the dominion of the Gentiles, it will be under them until the times of the Gentiles are fulfilled (v. 24c). The time during which the Gentiles have dominion will end when the Kingdom of Christ is established. From the Six Day War in 1967 until recently, Jerusalem has been under the total dominion of Israel, not the Gentiles. This tells us that Luke 21:24 is referring to a period of time at the very end, just before the Lord returns, as Revelation 11:2 confirms.

Since the beginning of the "Oslo War" in September 2000, it is no longer clear who has dominion over Jerusalem. Politicians say that Israel controls Jerusalem but what does *God* say? Jews are no longer permitted on the temple mount, the most important 50-acre area in the entire city. That area has been under the dominion of Yasser Arafat since 2000.

Maybe the Lord is referring to an even greater measure of Palestinian sovereignty (or some other Gentile sovereignty) over the entire Old City that is yet to come. We will soon know as events in the Middle East unfold. At the time of this writing, an alliance of the United States, Russia, the European Union, and the United Nations is attempting to force Israel to surrender its sovereignty over the Old City of Jerusalem to the Palestinians. This alliance is referred in the news media as "The Quartet." Their so-called "Roadmap to Peace" also requires Israel to abandon all the settlements and withdraw to its 1967 borders. According to Pentagon studies, those borders will leave Israel indefensible and lead to the demise of the nation. Could it be that Zechariah foresaw "The Quartet"? He speaks of four political powers or "horns" that will be used in the last days to scatter Israel (Zech. 1:18-19).

For many, it is not clear whether or not God presently considers Jerusalem to be under the dominion of the Gentiles. But either it is already under the Gentiles, or it will soon be under them and remain there until the Lord returns. While it is under them, God's people will

will experience the worst time of anguish in history. This time will end with the destruction of Jerusalem when not one stone will be left upon another within the city. In the context of that destruction, Jesus goes on to say in Luke 21:27-28:

> *27 And then shall they see the Son of man coming in a cloud with power and great glory.*
>
> *28 And when these things begin to come to pass, then look up, and lift up your heads; for your redemption draweth nigh.*

When we see the judgments and anguish on Israel that the Lord reveals in these verses, then He will come in the clouds (where we will meet Him, according to Paul), and our redemption will be at hand. To what "redemption" is He referring to here? Obviously, we are already redeemed in our spirits. But Paul tells us that all Christians are waiting for the "redemption" of our bodies (Rom. 8:23b). Christ's redemption of our physical bodies will be one of the blessings of the resurrection and rapture (I Cor. 15:51-54).

When we see these things begin to come to pass, we should look up and expectantly await the redemption of our bodies (Luke 21:28). The *first* thing that He tells us we will see is Jerusalem *"compassed with armies"* (Lk. 21:20a). When that happens, we should *"know that the desolation thereof is nigh"* (Lk. 21:20b). And when Jerusalem is destroyed, our redemption that will occur during the resurrection is near.

Is God's judgment on Jerusalem near? Some of the most powerful armies in history now surround Jerusalem and God's chosen people. Some of them are equipped with weapons of mass destruction, and their stated goal is the annihilation of the State of Israel. The nations whose armies are ready to strike Israel are Iraq, Syria, Iran, Saudi Arabia, Lebanon and the Palestinians. As we will see later, Jordan will also be involved in the coming war.

The delay will be short!

If our understanding is correct and the destruction of Israel is, in fact, the sign of the resurrection and rapture, then this important key should be confirmed in the Book of Revelation. In the next chapter, we will see that it is, in an amazingly clear way.

Chapter 12

Revelation Reveals the Sign of the Resurrection

Once we are able to determine with certainty who the great harlot is in Revelation 17-18, we will have an indisputable proof that the resurrection and rapture occur immediately after Jerusalem is destroyed. Most of us know that one of the traditional teachings on the last days declares that the harlot is Rome. If this is the case, then Peter's very important guideline for interpreting prophecy must be set aside. He wrote: *"Knowing this first, that no prophecy of the scripture is of any private interpretation"* (II Pet. 1:20).

This is the first thing Peter wants us to know and understand with regard to interpreting prophecy. If no one's personal interpretations are acceptable, then the only other option is to allow the Bible to interpret the Bible. The interpretation of every detail of every prophecy must be based on clear declarations of Scripture—so clear that they don't need our interpretations... so clear that they cannot be twisted.

Depending on how we count, there are somewhere between 40 and 60 details given about the great harlot in Revelation 17-18. The first big problem in believing that Rome is the harlot is that there is not a single Scripture anywhere in the Bible that directly and clearly links even one of these details to Rome. However, every one of these details are linked in Scripture to Jerusalem. For many, this might be a revolutionary thought, but let's consider just a little of the evidence.

Revelation 17:18 explains, *"... the woman which thou sawest is that great city."* In the context of the Book of Revelation itself we discover what city is the great city. Speaking of the bodies of the two witnesses we are told: *"And their dead bodies shall lie in the street of the great city, which spiritually is called Sodom and Egypt, where also our Lord was crucified "*(Rev. 11:8).

Speaking of the harlot, Revelation 18:24 reveals that *"... in her was found the blood of prophets, and of saints, and of all that were slain upon the earth."* It does not say that this harlot is guilty of "some" of the blood, but rather "all" of the blood of the prophets and saints. Some say that Rome is guilty of all the blood of the prophets and saints. One problem with this private interpretation is that Jesus tells Jerusalem *she* is guilty of *all* the blood of the prophets and saints shed upon the earth. It is not possible that two different cities are both guilty of this. Jesus gives us His interpretation in Matthew 23:33-37:

33 Ye serpents, ye generation of vipers, how can ye escape the damnation of hell?

34 Wherefore, behold, I send unto you prophets, and wise men, and scribes: and some of them ye shall kill and crucify; and some of them shall ye scourge in your synagogues, and persecute them from city to city:

*35 **That upon you may come all the righteous blood shed upon the earth, from the blood of righteous Abel unto the blood of Zacharias son of Barachias,** whom ye slew between the temple and the altar.*

36 Verily I say unto you, All these things shall come upon this generation.

*37 **O Jerusalem, Jerusalem, thou that killest the prophets, and stonest them which are sent unto thee, how often would I have gathered thy children together, even as a hen gathereth her chickens under her wings, and ye would not!***

Jesus said that the guilt of all the righteous blood shed *"shall come upon this generation"* (v. 36). By the word "generation," did He mean just the people alive in that day? Although the Greek word translated as "generation" can refer to a specific period of time, it also refers to a nation or a race of people. (See Strong's and Thayer's Greek Lexicons.) The guilt of all the righteous blood shed upon earth comes upon God's chosen people or His chosen race. Of course, all who repent are released from this guilt.

The blood of the "saints" is synonymous with the blood of the righteous, since both refer to God's people of faith. That blood comes on on Jerusalem (v. 35), who is also guilty of killing the prophets (v. 37). Most references to "Jerusalem" in the Bible are not referring to a natural city of streets and buildings. Buildings don't kill prophets. Most are referring to God's entire chosen people. This usage is still common today. When we speak of what "Moscow" has decided or what "London" has decided, we are not referring to cities with streets and buildings. We are referring to the Russians or the British. "Jerusalem" refers to God's people, Israel.

Isaiah 51:16-17 shows us that in the Bible Jerusalem refers to God's people: "... *say unto Zion, Thou art my people. Awake, awake, stand up, O Jerusalem...*"

Zion and Jerusalem in the Bible are synonymous (Heb. 12:22), so Jerusalem is His people. Isaiah 62:12 is another example of Jerusalem being a reference to God's people: "*And they shall call them, The holy people, The redeemed of the LORD: and thou shalt be called, Sought out, A city not forsaken.*"

Paul shows us the same truth in Galatians 4:25-28. However, he tells us that there are actually two Jerusalems, symbolic of two covenants and two peoples. Paul explains that the earthly or natural Jerusalem is symbolic of those who have been born only naturally—natural-born Jewish people. The other is heavenly Jerusalem that speaks of people born by spiritual means—the Church, the "mother of us all," or those who have been born again by the Spirit, both Jews and Gentiles. Paul's doctrine regarding the heavenly Jerusalem is confirmed in Revelation 21:2 where the "the holy city, the new Jerusalem" is used to refer to the entire Bride of Christ—God's holy nation made up of born-again Jews and Gentiles.

There is another, even greater problem with the private interpretation that teaches that Rome is the harlot... the very idea is an abomination and an affront to the Lord. Why? Let's suppose that throughout all of history there have been only two martyrs who have died for the true faith. One martyr was John Doe. He died in Rome. The other martyr was the Lord Jesus Christ. He died in Jerusalem. Which city is more guilty? Hopefully, no one would answer, "They are both just as guilty," since the Lord answers the question for us when He tells Capernaum that they are more guilty than Sodom (Matt. 11:23-24). Why is this so? Because the very Son of God spent time with them, showing them the truth and His glory, and they rejected Him. Sodom never had that opportunity.

Anyone who knows the Lord would declare that the city that killed the Son of God, the King of Glory, the only perfect Witness, would be more guilty than a city who rejected and killed an imperfect man who gave them an imperfect witness. Most would agree with this. However, let's add another martyr to our scales of justice, placing them on the side of Rome's guilt. We now have two men killed in Rome and only the Lord Jesus killed in Jerusalem. Are we willing to say that the two men outweigh, or are more important than the Lord? I trust not.

How many men would you have to add to *your* scales of justice before you would conclude that the men who died in Rome outweighed the importance of the Creator? Of one thing I am certain: the Father of the Lord Jesus Christ would never consider the sacrifices of men to be weightier or of more significance than what He and His Son did in Jerusalem. His evaluation of mankind is very clear—*"All nations before him are as nothing; and they are counted to him less than nothing, and vanity"* (Isa. 40:17). To hold up before the Lord the thousands of martyrs who died in Rome and tell Him that those men are more important than He, would be an abomination and an affront to Him!

The Bible tells us clearly in several places who is the great harlot. Speaking of Jerusalem, Isaiah laments, *"How is the faithful city become an harlot!"* (Isa. 1:21a) Ezekiel is a parallel message to the message found in the Book of Revelation; there are more than 30 major details found in both of these prophetic books. For example, they both begin with the same detailed vision of God's glory (Ezek. 1 and Rev. 4-5). Both men measure the temple. Both see people with a mark in their foreheads. Both eat the roll and it is sweet in their mouths and bitter in their bellies. Both see a great harlot. However, there is one small difference in the details about the harlot—Ezekiel tells us who she is—Jerusalem! (Ezek. 16)

One of the major reasons why there are so many contradictory interpretations of prophetic Scriptures is that they are often interpreted outside the context of the prophets of the Old Testament. Those men saw the end very clearly and often explained it in more detail than what we find in the New Testament. However, there is a tendency today to ignore them in favor of our own interpretations.

Some might say, "Yes, I see why some details of the harlot seem to speak of Jerusalem, but there are still too many details in Revelation 17-18 that just do not fit Jerusalem, but do seem to fit Rome." Let's consider a couple of those details. The problem is not that they don't fit

Jerusalem, but, rather, sometimes we need to compare what is being said more carefully with biblical and historical facts.

One example of a seeming conflict with Jerusalem being the harlot is that she *"reigneth over the kings of the earth"*(Rev. 17:18). Some may ask, "Does anyone believe that Jerusalem reigns over the kings of the earth?" Here, it is essential to keep in mind that "Jerusalem" refers to all of the Jewish people. Do the Jewish people reign over the kings of the earth? In this present world money rules, and most of the richest bankers on earth are Jews. Also, Jews invented some of the most powerful political movements in history. Karl Marx, the father of communism, was a Jew, and so was Lenin.

Billy Graham was recently vilified because of a tape recording, made many years ago, in which he made a statement to President Nixon while alone with him. Someone found it and revealed its contents in several major news publications. Many were deeply offended by it. In the recording, Billy Graham is heard lamenting the fact that the Jews controlled the news media of the world at that time. Anger over the statement cannot change the facts.

The reality of this world is that those who control the media have the power to make or break any political figure; they can almost choose which candidates will win elections. A better question would be, "Can anyone logically believe that Rome rules over the earth?" The Jews are under the covenant of Abraham, the heir of the world (Rom. 4:13). Is not that divine covenant still powerful? Rome is under nothing except a false religion and a deception. There is no power behind that!

What about all the filth and abominations that the harlot has spread around the world? Isn't Rome guilty of doing that? Rome's influence in promoting immorality doesn't compare to the filth that Hollywood has spread over the globe, and Jews own much of Hollywood.

Another detail about the harlot that many apply to Rome is that she is a city that sits on seven mountains (Rev. 17:9), and Rome is built on seven hills. However, the angel who was sent to John interprets the seven heads of the beast on which the woman sits. He explains, *"The seven heads are seven mountains, on which the woman sitteth. And there are seven kings... "*(Rev. 17:9b-10a).

Something that produces many false interpretations of prophecies is that we are prone to be inconsistent, especially when we want to prove a point. For example, a common mistake is to switch back and forth between a symbolic interpretation and a literal interpretation.

This has been done with the harlot and the seven mountains. We all know that the woman is a symbol of something or someone. She is not a literal woman. We all know that the beast is also symbolic; the harlot does not ride a literal beast. But suddenly, some declare that the seven mountains on which she sits are literal, natural mountains. This is not consistent interpretation.

In prophetic Scriptures, mountains are also symbolic. So let's continue the interpretation of the message about the harlot using symbolism throughout and not just in certain parts. Mountains are often used as a symbol of kings or kingdoms. For example, in Daniel 2:35 and 44, Daniel is interpreting Nebuchadnezzar's dream. He explains that the stone that smote the image "became a great mountain," and then he explains that the great mountain is a kingdom that shall endure forever. The Babylonian Empire is called a "destroying mountain" (Jer. 51:25).

Now the interpretation of the seven mountains that the angel gives to John makes sense. He tells him that the harlot sits on seven mountains, and *"there are seven kings... "* (Rev. 17:9b-10a). Throughout history, there have been seven empires (and *only* seven empires) that ruled during the history of the Jewish people. They are the Egyptian Empire, the Assyrian Empire, the Babylonian Empire, the Medo-Persian Empire, the Grecian Empire, the Roman Empire, and Islam. The Jewish people have managed to "ride" these empires to reach their goals in much the same way that a person rides a beast. In a few cases, it was even God's will for them to do so, as in the case of the Egyptian Empire, where Israel lived for many years.

In most cases, Israel paid a heavy price for using Gentile nations to reach her goals. Just as the beast the harlot rides has always done, in the end it will once again turn on her and destroy her (Rev. 17:16). From time to time throughout history the beast has done this to the harlot. For example, the harlot used Rome to reach her goals—to crucify the Lord and to imprison Paul. Later, Rome turned on Jerusalem and destroyed her in A.D. 70 and burned her with fire.

Two Important Prophetic Details

Before seeing why it is important to know who the harlot is, there are two issues that should be clarified.

First, in prophecy, kings and kingdoms are synonymous. For example, in Daniel 7:17, the angel tells Daniel that the four beasts are symbolic of four kings. But then, six verses later, within the same divine interpretation of the beasts, the angel tells Daniel that the fourth beast is a kingdom (Dan. 7:23). This is understandable because a kingdom is really an outgrowth of who and what its king is. That is why it matters greatly who our political leaders are. When the president is immoral, immorality fills the land.

Christ's Kingdom is certainly an outgrowth of who and what He is. The Kingdom of God is "righteousness, peace, and joy in the Holy Ghost" (Rom. 14:17). He is our righteousness; He is our peace; He is our joy. He is the Kingdom. No wonder we should seek first the Kingdom! (Matt. 6:33)

Second, many have taught that Babylon refers to the world system. This is an accurate conclusion and can be confirmed from Scripture. How, then, can Jerusalem be called Babylon? Ezekiel 23:14-18 exposes the sin of spiritual harlotry that Israel committed with the Babylonians when they chose them as spiritual lovers. Paul declares in I Corinthians 6:16, *"What? know ye not that he which is joined to an harlot is one body? for two, saith he, shall be one flesh."*

In using this verse to describe the result of Israel's harlotry with Babylon, some might be tempted to dismiss this powerful connection, saying that I Corinthians 6:16 is merely referring to the individual believer. It *is* referring to the individual believer, but this is also an immutable and indispensable truth and message throughout God's Word. God has *always* warned His people against both spiritual and literal harlotry, and its consequences for both an individual and a nation. (For further discussion on this, please refer to my book: *The Mystery: A Lost Key.*)

Jerusalem became one with the world system, Babylon, in much the same way that they became one with Sodom and Egypt. This is why He calls them spiritual Sodom and Egypt (Rev. 11:8), even though a literal Sodom and Egypt also existed. The same spiritual unity occurred in Israel when the leaders cried out, *"We have no king but Caesar"* (Jn. 19:15). They chose to become one with the Roman Empire that they so vehemently despised. God will look upon His own people as being one flesh with the world if they choose to be united to the world and live like the world. He will consider all those who walk in this way to be spiritual Babylon.

A Caution for Christians

Before any of us harshly criticize the Jewish people, a word of caution is in order for the so-called "Gentile Church." According to Paul, the Gentile believers were grafted into Israel, the olive tree (Rom. 11:17). However, from the beginning of the Bible, over and over God's people have actually produced two types of people. Adam produced a Cain and an Abel. Abraham produced an Ishmael and an Isaac. Jacob produced an Esau and a Jacob. These pairs of brothers all belonged to the same families and were symbolic of two ways—the way of the flesh and the way of the Spirit. Referring to Ishmael and Isaac, Paul clearly points this out in Galatians 4:29.

In addition to the symbolism seen in these brothers, we find a number of biblical examples where men of faith had two wives living in the same house. Abraham, Jacob, and Elkanah each had two wives. Paul also gives us insight into what this biblical thread of truth reveals. In Galatians he explains that Abraham had two wives and through them gave birth to two sons. Paul explains that these pairs are symbolic of two covenants, two peoples, two mountains, and two Jerusalems (Gal. 4:21-31, NKJV).

The families of some of history's greatest men of faith had two types of sons, and some of the greatest men of faith also had two wives. Is it possible that this a problem in God's spiritual family also—in His Church? As we have seen, Peter and Jude speak about false brethren being found inside the Church, specifically in the last days. The Church is God's house and His family. It seems to be more than a coincidence that at the end of God's Word we are shown two women, the harlot in Revelation 17-18 and the Bride of Christ, or *heavenly* Jerusalem in Revelation 21:2. We have already seen that the Bible associates the harlot with *earthly* Jerusalem. So both of the Jerusalems that Paul mentions are found in Revelation. What is the message?

During the first coming of Christ, two different types of people were produced by the Jewish nation... those who rejected the Lord and crucified Him, and those who loved Him and became His disciples. In other words, there were those who chose the way of the flesh and became identified with the earthly Jerusalem that is guilty of all the righteous blood shed. And there were those who chose the way of the Spirit and became identified with the heavenly Jerusalem.

As believers, the Gentiles cannot declare on one hand that they have been grafted into Israel, and on the other hand that all the evil found

found in the harlot is associated only with the natural-born Jews. The problem is that *all* of God's people, Jews and Gentiles, are part of His house; *all* are choosing either the way of the flesh or the way of the Spirit on a daily basis; all are either seeking after power, money, pleasures and things of this world or they are seeking after the Lord and His will.

The nature of the harlot is to oppress the righteous, and that nature is not only found among the Jewish people of God. For the last 2,000 years, the harlot's nature has also been found among the Gentile people of God. Jews did not imprison John Bunyan for preaching on the streets of Bedford, England. Jews did not burn John Huss at the stake. Jews did not oppress millions in the Inquisitions. Gentiles who called themselves "Christians" did all these things and many more during the last 2000 years. In every case, unless those Gentiles repented of their ways, they, too ended their lives being included in the company that God calls a harlot, just as surely as did the Pharisees who crucified the Lord. In short, anyone who calls himself a follower of the God of Israel but chooses to live for this world and the flesh runs the risk of being gathered with the harlot system in the day of judgment. That harlot system includes all Jews and Gentiles who choose the way of Cain, Baalam, and Korah.

The Condition of the World
Is a Reflection of the Church

Most Christians bewail the condition of the world today. The schools are filled with drugs, alcohol, immorality, rebellion and even murder. We have attempted to make everything childproof except our schools, the place where our children spend a large portion of their lives. Naturally and spiritually, schools are very unsafe for children. Living in the nations of the world is also unsafe. The governments of the world are filled with corruption; violence fills our streets; hatred and divorce fill our homes. Superterrorism now hangs over our heads like a cloud. Instead of knowing God's cloud and His blessing, we live under Satan's cloud and his curse.

What is wrong? Is this happening simply because mankind is destined to end this way? The Lord gave His Church an answer to this question by means of the Welsh revival that occurred near the beginning of the twentieth century. Wales was an ungodly nation filled with miners who could only think of drinking, swearing, immorality, and dirty jokes. There seemed to be little hope. But one day Pastor Evan Roberts started to pray before his Sunday morning message. The Spirit of God came upon him and the only thing he could cry out was, "Lord, bend us!" He prayed this over and over until, after a time, the people began to pray the same thing.

The spirit of repentance began to flow in the church, and then out into the streets. People who had never attended church before began to come into the services under great conviction, crying out for forgiveness. The river of God's presence began to flow to other cities of Wales. Within a period of about three months, most of the taverns and cinemas of the entire nation were permanently closed! The miners were going to the mines singing hymns instead of telling dirty jokes. The nation was transformed by one mighty visitation of God that came through broken and repentant hearts.

The Lord is well able to do the same thing today in any nation on earth. If we find grace in God's eyes, His glory will fall upon us in such a mighty way, and His voice will be heard once again in the earth with such power that sinners will fear God instead of mocking Him. Instead of "coming out," homosexuals will either slither back into the darkness in shame or repent and turn to God. Discotheques and nightclubs will close due to a lack of customers. Neighborhoods will be changed from being the domain of drug pushers to being the domain of youth who seek the Lord. Instead of handing out drugs, they will hand out tracts. Homes will be restored and spouses who fought with one another will now pray with one another. God is well able to convince a sinner of his sin, but can He find a Church that will wholly surrender to Him? The world is lost today because the Church has a name that it lives but is dead (Rev. 3:1). May the Lord rescue every one of us from our lethargy and lukewarmness before it is too late.

The Rapture Occurs When the Great Harlot Is Destroyed

The details concerning the judgment on the great harlot in Revelation 18 are actually further confirmation that she is symbolic of God's people, Israel, who have turned away from Him. The Lord always begins His judgments with His own house, and the natural house of Israel is where the cleansing will begin. Consider the following:

In Revelation 18:4b, the Lord exhorts: *"... Come out of her, my people, that ye be not partakers of her sins, and that ye receive not of her plagues."*

Paul tells us there will be a remnant saved in natural Israel (Rom. 9:3-4, 27); there are true people of God within the nation of Israel. God has not rejected Israel (Rom. 11:1-5), and He never will (Jer. 31:35-36; 33:24-26). He loves the nation enough to discipline and purify them (Heb. 12:6). The above exhortation to come out from among those who will be judged is an echo of the Lord's exhortation in Matthew 24. This is the only other place in the Bible where the Lord gives a general exhortation to His people to flee from a specific place. There, He exhorts those who are in Judea to flee because of the great tribulation that will come upon them (Matt. 24:15-21).

Revelation 18:6: *"Reward her even as she rewarded you, and double unto her double according to her works... "*

The only people in all the Bible who receive double for their sins is Jerusalem, as Isaiah 40:2 declares:

"Speak ye comfortably to Jerusalem, and cry unto her, that her warfare is accomplished, that her iniquity is pardoned: for she hath received of the LORD'S hand double for all her sins."

Revelation confirms Paul's message that sudden destruction will come upon Jerusalem:

"Therefore shall her plagues come in one day... "(Rev. 18:8a).

"... for in one hour is thy judgment come... "(Rev. 18:10).

"For in one hour so great riches is come to nought... "(Rev. 18:17a).

"... for in one hour is she made desolate."(Rev. 18:19b)

The following verse causes many to reject the idea that the harlot is Jerusalem. We are told:

"And a mighty angel took up a stone like a great millstone, and cast it into the sea, saying, Thus with violence shall that great city Babylon be thrown down, and shall be found no more at all." (Rev. 18:21)

We need to recall what Paul tells us in Galatians 4:24-28. There are two Jerusalems. One is earthly and the other is heavenly. One is carnal and comes from Hagar, the *Egyptian*. This is one reason why the earthly Jerusalem is called spiritual *Egypt* (Rev. 11:8). She is the one who

who crucified the Lord and who lives for this world, for honor and position, and for the flesh. Her children are born after the flesh and persecute those who are born after the Spirit (Gal. 4:29). She will cease to exist and finally, the heavenly Jerusalem will descend to earth and remain on earth forever, just as is seen happening in Revelation 21:2-3. What a day that will be!

Let's see what happens immediately after Jerusalem is destroyed as recorded in Revelation 19:1-9:

1 And after these things I heard a great voice of much people in heaven, saying, Alleluia; Salvation, and glory, and honour, and power, unto the Lord our God:

2 For true and righteous are his judgments: for he hath judged the great whore, which did corrupt the earth with her fornication, and hath avenged the blood of his servants at her hand.

3 And again they said, Alleluia. And her smoke rose up for ever and ever.

4 And the four and twenty elders and the four beasts fell down and worshipped God that sat on the throne, saying, Amen; Alleluia.

5 And a voice came out of the throne, saying, Praise our God, all ye his servants, and ye that fear him, both small and great.

6 And I heard as it were the voice of a great multitude, and as the voice of many waters, and as the voice of mighty thunderings, saying, Alleluia: for the Lord God omnipotent reigneth.

7 Let us be glad and rejoice, and give honour to him: for the marriage of the Lamb is come, and his wife hath made herself ready.

8 And to her was granted that she should be arrayed in fine linen, clean and white: for the fine linen is the righteousness of saints.

9 And he saith unto me, Write, Blessed are they which are called unto the marriage supper of the Lamb. And he saith unto me, These are the true sayings of God.

After the great harlot is judged, the Lord's Bride is taken to the Marriage Supper by means of the resurrection and rapture. So, Revelation confirms in a very clear way that the resurrection and rapture will occur immediately after Jerusalem is destroyed. We have seen that the destruction of Israel is at hand. Therefore, the coming of the Lord is at hand. The delay will be short.

At this point, some might observe, "Earlier you wrote that the resurrection and rapture occur in Revelation 10:7, and now you are saying they occur in Revelation 19." A careful reading of the Book of Revelation shows that the message of the last days is repeated in the Book. Almost every detail appears two times. First, the heavenly messenger reveals the end to John. His message is based on the contents of a little book. Afterward, John eats the book and it becomes part of him. After assimilating the message, John then prophesies that same message, but obviously in his own words (Rev. 10:8-11). Every word or message from God must be confirmed in the mouth of two or three witnesses (II Cor. 13:1). This is especially true for a message so momentous as that given in the Book of Revelation, so the Lord confirmed it by giving it through both the heavenly messenger and John.

As confirmation, here is a partial comparison between the first half of Revelation and the latter half, showing how the message is repeated in the Book:

1. **Revelation 5:6**—There is a revelation of the Lamb in this vision.
   Revelation 14:1—There is a revelation of the Lamb in this vision.

2. **Revelation 7:1-8**—There is a revelation of 144,000 sealed ones.
   Revelation 14:1—There is a revelation of 144,000 sealed ones.

3. **Revelation 7:3**—They are sealed in their foreheads.
   Revelation 14:1—They are sealed in their foreheads.

4. **Revelation 4:1**—A voice is heard from Heaven.
   Revelation 14:2—A voice is heard from Heaven.

5. **Revelation 4:5**—Thunder is heard.
   Revelation 14:2—Thunder is heard.

6. **Revelation 5:9**—A new song is heard.
   Revelation 14:3—A new song is heard.

7. **Revelation 4:2-3**—There is a revelation of the throne of God.
   Revelation 14:3—There is a revelation of the throne of God.

8. **Revelation 4:6**—Four "beasts," or four living creatures, are seen.
   Revelation 14:3—Four "beasts," or four living creatures, are seen.

9. **Revelation 4:4**—The elders are seen.
   Revelation 14:3—The elders are seen.

10. **Revelation 7:10-12**—This multitude is worshipping the Lord.
    Revelation 15:3-4—This multitude is worshipping the Lord.

11. **Revelation 8:4**—In this context smoke fills the Temple.
    Revelation 15:8—In this context smoke fills the Temple.

Compare the Seven Trumpets and the Seven Vials

12. **Revelation 8:7**—TRUMPET ONE deals with the earth.
    Revelation 16:2—VIAL ONE deals with the earth.

13. **Revelation 8:8**—TRUMPET TWO deals with the sea.
    Revelation 16:3—VIAL TWO deals with the sea.

14. **Revelation 8:10**—TRUMPET THREE deals with rivers.
    Revelation 16:4—VIAL THREE deals with rivers.

15. **Revelation 8:12**—TRUMPET FOUR deals with the sun.
    Revelation 16:8—VIAL FOUR deals with the sun.

16. **Revelation 9:1-3,5**—TRUMPET FIVE deals with darkness and pain.
    Revelation 16:10—VIAL FIVE deals with darkness and pain.

17. **Revelation 9:14**—TRUMPET SIX deals with the Euphrates River.
    Revelation 16:12—VIAL SIX deals with the Euphrates River.

18. **Revelation 10:7 and 11:15-19**—TRUMPET SEVEN is associated with ten details:

    1. Revelation 10:7 and 11:15—The seventh angel is involved.
    2. Revelation 11:15—There were great voices in Heaven.
    3. Revelation 11:15—The kingdoms of the world are taken.
    4. Revelation 11:18—Man's anger is seen.
    5. Revelation 11:18—God's wrath comes upon man.
    6. Revelation 11:19—There is a revelation of the Temple.
    7. Revelation 11:19—Lightning accompanies the seventh trumpet.
    8. Revelation 11:19—Thunder accompanies the seventh trumpet.
    9. Revelation 11:19—An earthquake accompanies the seventh trumpet.
    10. Revelation 11:19—A great hail accompanies the seventh trumpet.

Revelation 16:17-21—VIAL SEVEN is associated with ten details. The same ten details are related to both the seventh vial and seventh trumpet. Therefore, they must refer to the same event.

1. Revelation 16:17—The seventh angel is involved.
2. Revelation 16:17-18—There is a great voice and voices are in Heaven.
3. Revelation 16:19—The kingdoms of the world are taken (as seen by the fall of the capital city, Babylon, and the cities, which are governmental centers).
4. Revelation 16:21—Man's anger is seen.
5. Revelation 16:19—God's wrath comes upon man.
6. Revelation 16:17—There is a revelation of the Temple.
7. Revelation 16:18—Lightning accompanies the seventh vial.
8. Revelation 16:18—Thunder accompanies the seventh vial.
9. Revelation 16:18—An earthquake accompanies the seventh vial.
10. Revelation 16:21—A great hail accompanies the seventh vial.

19. **Revelation 12:1**—Immediately after the seventh trumpet, and the ten things associated with it, there is a revelation of a woman.

    Revelation 17:1—Immediately after the seventh vial, and the ten things associated with it, there is a revelation of a woman. The Holy Spirit makes twelve very clear contrasts between these two women. (This is discussed in detail in my book, *The Final Victory: The Year 2000?*, pp. 128-130.)

20. **Revelation 10:7**—We previously demonstrated that after the seventh trumpet the Church is raptured and carried to the Marriage Supper. The repeated sequence of events in Revelation confirms that since the rapture is found in Revelation 19:7-9 at this point, the rapture must also occur at this point in the first half of Revelation — as it does in Revelation 10:7.

    Revelation 19:7-9—After the seventh vial, the Bride is taken to the Marriage Supper.

Chapter 13

Who Will Destroy Israel?

Referring to Ishmael, the son of Abraham, the Lord described the worldwide infamy that Ishmael would one day attain, saying, *"And he will be a wild man; his hand will be against every man, and every man's hand against him..."* (Gen. 16:12) After the destruction of the World Trade Center on September 11, 2001, Osama bin Laden declared, "Today, Islam is against the world and the world is against Islam." Is there any connection between the Lord's description of Ishmael being against the world and the world against Ishmael and the words of bin Laden?

Osama bin Laden is a descendent of Ishmael, as are most of the people in Saudi Arabia, the ancestral home of Ishmael's descendents. Most of the 19 hijackers who participated in the attack on the United States were Saudi Arabian citizens. But bin Laden did not say that Saudi Arabia is against the world, but rather, that Islam is against the world. Islam is a religion that was founded by a descendent of Ishmael—Mohammad, who was born and raised in Mecca, Saudi Arabia.

Islam was founded by descendents of Ishmael, and it exalts Ishmael, claiming that *he*, rather than Isaac, is the rightful heir of the promises that God made to Abraham. Islam even claims that it was Ishmael whom Abraham offered to God on the altar. Islam has not only embraced Ishmael, but it has imbibed his spirit and nature. Islam's writings and history amply confirm this. The Lord called John the Baptist "Elijah" because he carried the spirit of Elijah (Lk. 1:17). For the same reason we can call Islam "Ishmael"—because it carries the wild spirit of Ishmael.

Romans 4:13 gives understanding of a core issue regarding God's promises to Abraham and what is at stake: *"For the promise, that he should be the heir of the world, was not to Abraham, or to his seed, through the law, but through the righteousness of faith."*

God has promised that Abraham and his descendents will inherit the whole world. The Bible proclaims that this promise will be fulfilled through Jesus Christ, a descendent of Abraham through Isaac's lineage. Jesus Christ is also the Son of God because He was birthed by God the Father through the work of the Holy Spirit and raised from the dead by the Holy Spirit (Rom. 1:3-4; Lu. 1:34-35; Acts 13:33). The Father has appointed His Son, Jesus Christ, as the heir of all things (Heb. 1:2).

Receiving the entire world as an inheritance is not only a core issue in God's promise to Abraham but it is a core issue in the worldwide conflict that is unfolding at this moment. This conflict began 4,000 years ago between Ishmael and Isaac. What is being decided on the world scene today is which of Abraham's sons is the rightful heir to the whole world. Either Ishmael and his descendents will inherit the earth or else Isaac and his descendents will do so. The Bible declares unequivocally that the promise will be fulfilled through Isaac. Paul wrote about the battle between Ishmael and Isaac and how they were birthed by two mothers, Hagar and Sarah. He declared:

Now we, brethren, as Isaac was, are the children of promise. But as then he that was born after the flesh persecuted him that was born after the Spirit, even so it is now. Nevertheless what saith the scripture? Cast out the bondwoman and her son: for the son of the bondwoman shall not be heir with the son of the freewoman. (Gal. 4:28-30)

Abraham made a catastrophic mistake in following the advice of Sarah, his barren wife, to have a son through Hagar, their slave. After Hagar's son, Ishmael, was born, Abraham paid an enormous price for about 15 years while Hagar and Ishmael lived in his house. The recriminations, conflict, and intrigue that filled his home are described in Genesis 16. But this is nothing compared with the price that Abraham's natural and spiritual descendents have paid for about 4,000 years. The Jewish people and the Christian world are once again facing the onslaughts of Ishmael's descendents.

The words and actions of Osama bin Laden, Saddam Hussein, Yasser Arafat, the Ayatollah Khomeini, government leaders of Saudi Arabia (who have just recently been exposed for supporting worldwide terrorism), and many others reveal a well defined goal—world conquest in the name of Ishmael's religion. This is not the first time that the spirit of Ishmael has attempted to conquer the world but it will be the last, because the rightful heir, the Lord Jesus Christ, will soon ascend His throne and rule over the whole earth!

Yes, Abraham made a mistake when he birthed Ishmael but that mistake did not cause God to change His mind nor to rescind His promises to Abraham. Our God is a God of mercy, forgiveness and restoration. He is also sovereign and has decreed that Abraham and his descendents through Isaac will inherit the earth (Rom. 9:6-9). Nothing will ever change this divine decree. Biblically, these descendents include all Jews and Gentiles who have placed their faith in the Redeemer of mankind (Gal. 3:28-29). No wonder there is so much anti-Semitism and anti-Christian right in the world today. The god of this world knows who will soon take his kingdom!

Some Christians have accepted the tragic error that teaches that the God of the Bible and the god of Islam are the same God, and that Islam is a peace-loving religion. The nature of Islam is the nature of Ishmael because it sprang from him, and that nature precludes Islam being a peace-loving religion. (For more details on the nature of Islam, please refer to *Yasser Arafat—An Apocalyptic Character?*, pp. 31-62.) Islam promotes the wild nature that the Lord said would characterize Ishmael.

If flying airplanes into skyscrapers or donning explosive belts and blowing one's own self up on public buses is not wild, then what is? Actions of this nature, repeated somewhere in the world almost daily, coupled with history and the so-called "holy books" of Islam prove that Islam is not a peace-loving religion, nor is the god of Islam our God. Jesus said, *"By their fruits ye shall know them"* (Matt. 7:20), and these actions, considered "noble" by Islam, reveal Islam's source. How could anyone conclude that the God Who created the flowers for our joy and Who sends His blessings on the just and the unjust could also be the god of Islam? Jesus taught that His disciples should win the world through love; Mohammad taught that his disciples should win the world through slaughter and death. Is your God the author of both these religions?

Some would counter, "But the Islamic fanatics who are warring against the world are not true representatives of Islam or its god." History tells us that Mohammad entered a stone house in Mecca where there were many demonic idols. He destroyed all the idols except one and declared that the one he spared would be the god of Islam. Mohammad wrote in the *Koran* that the god of Islam "loves those who fight in his cause in battle array..." (Sura 61:4). He also condemned pacifists, writing, "O ye who believe! what is the matter with you, that, when ye are asked to go forth in the cause of Allah, ye cling heavily to the earth?... Unless ye go forth, he will punish you with a grievous penalty, and put others in your place" (Sura 9:38-39). As recorded in Islam's second holy book, *The Hadith*, Mohammad also declared, "You will fight against the Jews and you will kill them until even a stone would say, 'Come here, Muslim, there is a Jew (hiding himself behind me) [sic]; kill him' " (Siddiqi's translation of *The Hadith*, p. 1510).

It is easy to discern the infinite difference between the Judeo-Christian faith and the Islamic faith. It is also easy to see that these faiths do not proceed from the same God. The Spirit of the true God that lived in the Apostle Paul revealed His attitude toward the Jews. God's Spirit inspired in Paul such a love for the Jews that he was willing to give his own life for them (Rom. 9:1-4). Which god is it, then, who would say that the Muslims should kill all the Jews? Only the god who comes to kill, steal, and destroy—Satan, the god of this world.

Both Mohammad's teachings and the deadly fruit that has grown out of them expose their spiritual source. Mohammad lived his own message, and his followers have done the same. Just as Mohammad slaughtered all the males of the Kuraish tribe because they would not convert to Islam, history is replete with examples of Muslims slaughtering the infidels (often Christians) who would not convert to Islam.

What Islam has done to the Jews throughout history and what Islam is doing to the Jews today should give us the clue we need to know who will destroy Israel. Yasser Arafat is a descendent of Mohammad. At an early age he devoured and memorized the teachings of the *Koran* with such mastery that his principal teacher concluded that Yasser was a supernatural child with a supernatural call. In those days, fervent Muslims believed their god's "call" was to destroy all the Jews on earth. This is still on their agenda, but that agenda has been whitewashed and hidden, even from the eyes of Western political leaders.

Islam's agenda is so carefully hidden by the Western media that followers of Islam were able to carry out over 15,000 terrorist attacks against the tiny nation of Israel between September 2000 and February 2003. This adds up to more than one attack every hour and a half for two and a half years! If any other nation on earth were experiencing this, it would use all the military capability at its disposal to eliminate its enemies.

Israel has the capability to destroy her enemies, but if she accidentally kills a civilian in her quest to defend herself, the condemnation of the international community usually appears the next day on the front pages of most major newspapers. The U.N. frequently issues a resolution condemning Israel if an Islamic civilian dies in the conflict. There is relatively little reaction in the world community against Yasser Arafat and his thugs when they attack a school bus and kill Israeli children. The world has always given the Jewish people the right to die but not the right to defend themselves.

Some may conclude that Arafat's attacks against Israel are not really a manifestation of Islam. However, for at least two years, Saddam Hussein has given $25,000 to each family that has provided a suicide bomber who succeeded in carrying out an attack against Israel. Iran, Saudi Arabia, Lebanon, Sudan, Libya, and many other countries not only support these attacks with their words but also with their money, giving financial help, training, and sanctuary to terrorist groups who are involved in liberating Palestine in the name of Islam.

Why isn't the world screaming about this injustice? Because the Islamic world controls most of the world's oil reserves, and for most people and nations, the bottom line is money. And, incidentally, who put all that oil under their control? God did. The same God who foresaw what Ishmael would end up doing to the world and revealed that Ishmael would one day be against the whole world. This is all part of the divine plan to expose what is really in man's heart and to bring in His eternal Kingdom.

The present administration of the United States government has mistakenly declared that we are not in a war against Islam. Unfortunately, if the United States is a true ally of Israel, this declaration is simply not true. Just as unfortunate is the fact that all *true* disciples of Islam see things from a different perspective, as Osama bin Laden made clear when he said that Islam is now fighting against all the earth. Millions of true Muslims are willing to fight against all Judeo-Christian values and beliefs until they either obtain victory or are dead. The non-Islamic world is not dealing with what the Western media call "a handful of Islamic fundamentalist fanatics." We are dealing with millions of fervent disciples of Mohammad who are willing to lay down their lives as they slaughter the world's infidels.

The world will soon discover that the core issue today regarding war and peace is that God's promise to Abraham is a far more weighty matter than most are willing to acknowledge. God and religion cannot be divorced from reality as many governments have attempted to do. God and His Word will endure and succeed long after all the nations of the earth cease to exist (and they will, in fact, cease to exist as Jeremiah 46:27-28 reveals). According to Jesus, the "times of the Gentiles" will come to an end (Lu. 21:24). The earmark of these times is the governmental rule of the Gentiles (Mk. 10:42). Someone other than Gentiles will soon rule the world.

God has decreed that His people from all ages will inherit and rule over the Earth with Christ as the head of His worldwide Kingdom (Rev. 2:25-26; Eph. 1:22-23). The descendents of Ishmael are not willing to sit back and allow this to come to pass without bringing to bear on the world the full force of the battle that Ishmael initiated against Isaac in Genesis. They perceive that the best way to thwart this plan is to destroy God's chosen people, the Jews and Christians, and to take control of God's Land. To do this, they must also destroy Israel's only real ally, the nation they have designated as "The Great Satan"—the United States. Islam's final battle has begun, and soon they will war against the Lamb and His saints on Mount Zion, but the Lamb will prevail!

The Ten Horns Destroy the Harlot

God calls His chosen people, Israel, a harlot in both the Old and New Testaments. His people are guilty of spiritual harlotry in departing from their God and running after other lovers. However, the Lord promises to restore His glory and righteousness to His people in the last days. To accomplish this, the Lord will bring severe discipline on Israel, allowing her to be crushed. Revelation tells us plainly who will be used to bring judgment on the harlot.

In Revelation 17:16, the great harlot is judged by the ten horns found on a beast. We are told that the ten horns represent ten kings, or ten nations (Rev. 17:12). There are differences of opinion in the Church today about which nations these horns represent. A study of these horns is outside the scope of this book. However, if we adhere to Peter's guidelines concerning prophecy, then our own private interpretations should be exchanged for what the Bible shows us clearly. According to Daniel 7-8, these ten horns occupy part of the territory that was conquered by the first king of the Grecian Empire, Alexander the Great.

Alexander's conquests involved the lands between Greece and India. He never pushed west into Europe. Since all of this territory is presently under Islam, we can be certain that it will be Islamic nations who will be used to crush Israel. (For a biblical basis to determine who these ten horns are, please refer to my book, *Yasser Arafat—An Apocalyptic Character?*, pp. 13-16)

In Psalm 83 there are ten nations mentioned whose avowed purpose is the destruction of Israel. The modern nations that those biblical names encompass are Iraq, Syria, Iran, Saudi Arabia, Jordan, Lebanon, and the Palestinians. All of these were named as allies in the 1996 report from the Task Force on Terrorism and Unconventional Warfare mentioned earlier. That report predicted the destruction of Israel as a result of an attack from these nations.

The last two verses of Psalm 83 are like prophetic signposts to show us that this Psalm is speaking about events which will occur in the last days. These ten nations will be troubled forever; they will perish, and at that time they will know that the Lord is God over all the earth (v. 17-18, NKJV). Far from knowing that the God of Israel is the God of all the earth, all these nations are presently under the deception of Islam. In fact, few nations on earth would be so prone to make war against the Lord and against His saints as would the nations of the Islamic world. The ten horns will fight against the Lord Himself according to Revelation 17:14.

There are some very astounding facts surrounding the current Middle East scenario. First, 80 years ago, not a single nation existed there. Almost the entire area was under the British Mandate and consisted of one huge tract of land. Before Israel and the other nations of the Middle East had been restored, anyone who read and understood the message of the prophets was confronted with two choices regarding many prophecies. They either had to engage in a tremendous amount of spiritualization of the events described by the prophets, assuming that everything was merely symbolic, or else they had to recognize that the Lord's coming was not at hand.

The prophets wrote about what Israel, Syria, the Palestinians (Philistines), the Egyptians, the Assyrians, etc. would do in the last days. None of those nations even existed, so how could the prophecies related to them have been fulfilled? Of course, before these nations were restored, many who read the prophets chose to engage in elaborate spiritualizations of the prophecies about those nations. Those private interpretations have proven to be hollow; what the prophets saw is now coming to pass *precisely* and *literally*.

The biblical nations of the Middle East have all been resurrected out of the dust, so to speak. They are now a reality, and the words of the prophets are being fulfilled in a very literal way. Revelation 17:12 explains that these ten horns will have power for only one hour in the last days. Most of the Islamic nations of the Middle East are less than 80 years old. They have received power for a very short time in these last days.

Is all this merely a series of coincidences, or is God fulfilling His prophetic word regarding the ten horns, the nation of Israel, and His coming? Since the coming of the Lord will occur when Israel is destroyed, and since the ten horns will be used to destroy Israel, it seems clear that the delay in the Lord's coming will be very short. The ten horns exist today, and they all have a burning desire to destroy Israel.

What About the "Little Horn"?

No discussion of Israel's enemies is complete without mentioning Yasser Arafat. He has killed more Jews than any other man alive today. For many years, Israel has considered him to be its worst enemy. I believe Mr. Arafat, in his position, is the "little horn" described by Daniel the prophet. Arafat has fulfilled most of the things that Daniel said the little horn would do in the last days, as I explain in my book, *Yasser Arafat—An Apocalyptic Character?*

Although some have concluded that the little horn is a worldwide antichrist who will have power over every nation on earth, Daniel calls him "little." Daniel mentions a number of political leaders in his prophecy, calling them "horns." He uses the size of each of those horns as a measure of the extent of power each leader wields (e.g., Dan. 8). Surely, the kingdom of the little horn is not greater than the kingdom of the biggest horn in Daniel's prophecy, seen to be the first king of the Grecian Empire (Dan. 8:5, 21). That king was Alexander the Great who ruled over the lands between Greece and India; he did not even rule over the whole known world, much less over the whole earth.

Arafat is the leader of a very little people, the Palestinians. Although they too will have a part in Israel's destruction, the little horn and his people do not play a major role in that destruction. In fact, Daniel 11:45 shows that the little horn goes out with a whimper—*"... he shall come to his end, and none shall help him."*

Interestingly, for nine months, between April 2002 and February 2003, Israel did not allow Arafat to leave Ramallah. They destroyed his entire office complex there except for the two rooms in which Arafat has been living during all these months. No one is helping him. He is either coming to his end or will very soon be resurrected, politically speaking.

From God's perspective, Jerusalem might already be under the dominion of the Gentiles to the degree that the Lord had in mind when He described the end. Arafat has controlled the temple mount since September of 2000. If this is the control the Lord was referring to, then the end of Israel and the Lord's coming are both very near.

On the other hand, if a greater degree of sovereignty over the Old City is what the Lord was foretelling, then Arafat (or else his successor, if Arafat dies), and the Palestinians are likely to be resurrected politically once again. If so, the Palestinian leader will be given a greater degree of sovereignty over Jerusalem than he presently has (possibly even complete sovereignty). If this occurs, then the last three and a half years before the Lord's return will begin with that event and Israel's destruction will occur at the end of that period, as Daniel 12 explains. Also, the terrible time of sorrows that the Jewish people have been experiencing since September of 2000 will prove to be only a prelude to what will yet occur. If this is the case, may the Lord show mercy to His remnant, and may we be faithful to pray for the peace of Jerusalem!

Chapter 14

How Will We Respond to Israel's Destruction?

Lest we approach the subject of Israel's destruction with triviality or lightness, may the Lord allow us to know His heart toward His people and His holy city, Jerusalem. In the hour of Israel's judgment, some will weep, some will rejoice and many, including Christians, will ask, "Where is their God?" The world will incorrectly conclude that either the God of Israel has forsaken His people or, worse, that He doesn't even exist. The Lord loves Israel with an everlasting love. For that reason, the coming fires of judgment upon Israel will bring Him great sorrow. However, an even greater sorrow for the Lord will be the reproach and stigma that His own name and reputation will suffer at the hands of mankind, as a result of Israel's destruction.

Almost all of us are very concerned about our reputations. The Lord is also concerned about His name or reputation. But there is an enormous difference between His motive for protecting His reputation and our motive for protecting ours. Our concern is usually motivated by pride, ambition and self-interest. He protects His because *"there is none other name under heaven given among men, whereby [man] must be saved"*(Acts 4:12). He does so because of His love for man rather than because of pride or self-love. If His name is despised and mocked, He knows that multitudes among the nations will end in hell.

Yet, because of His great love for Israel, His "firstborn" (Exod. 4:22), He is willing to discipline him even at the risk of His own reputation, and even though the world will not understand what is happening. When I have taught on Israel's coming judgment, a frequent question is, "Are you saying that God is gathering the Jews from among the nations in order to kill them?" I am only saying what the Lord Himself tells us in Ezekiel, a book that deals with Israel in the last days. Ezekiel 22:18-22 tells us:

18 Son of man, the house of Israel is to me become dross: all they are brass, and tin, and iron, and lead, in the midst of the furnace; they are even the dross of silver.

19 Therefore thus saith the Lord GOD; Because ye are all become dross, behold, therefore I will gather you into the midst of Jerusalem.

20 As they gather silver, and brass, and iron, and lead, and tin, into the midst of the furnace, to blow the fire upon it, to melt it; so will I gather you in mine anger and in my fury, and I will leave you there, and melt you.

21 Yea, I will gather you, and blow upon you in the fire of my wrath, and ye shall be melted in the midst thereof.

22 As silver is melted in the midst of the furnace, so shall ye be melted in the midst thereof; and ye shall know that I the LORD have poured out my fury upon you.

Ezekiel was in the Babylonian captivity when he wrote this. This was not a prophecy about God's future judgment on Israel by means of the Babylonians; that judgment had already fallen. It could not be referring to the attack on Jerusalem under the Romans in A.D. 70, because the Lord did not "gather" the Jews at that time. They had been brought back from Babylon over 600 years prior to that attack. They were already in the Holy Land and were actually scattered by Titus. It can only be referring to a future furnace of purification.

We are living in the day when He has gathered His people from the nations, but their way of living is a reproach to His Name and also a reproach to many people who do not even know the Lord. Having lived in Israel for two and a half years, my wife and I are witnesses of the gross immorality and sin among His people. This is reflected in many ways, but one example is in the dress code of many of the women and young girls. Their dress is more immoral than anything we have faced anywhere else in the world. Although Islam is engaged in an evil and unjustified spiritual battle against Israel, their abhorrence of the immoral dress code of many Israelis is justified. The Lord is going to respond, but we should also respond by weeping for the nation.

Moses also spoke of Israel's cleansing and travail in the last days. He wrote:

> *When thou art in tribulation, and all these things are come upon thee, even in the latter days, if thou turn to the LORD thy God, and shalt be obedient unto his voice; (For the LORD thy God is a merciful God;) he will not forsake thee, neither destroy thee, nor forget the covenant of thy fathers which he sware unto them.* (Deut. 4:30-31)

The Lord loves His people and will do whatever is necessary to bring them back to Himself, even at the risk of His own Name. But He also loves Jerusalem, the city He has chosen from among the nations. To us, as Christians, how important is Jerusalem today? Does Jerusalem mean anything to you? Is it no longer important that the Lord will literally reign some day soon from His holy mountain, Jerusalem? Does it matter that *"at that time Jerusalem shall be called The Throne of the Lord, and all the nations shall be gathered to it, to the name of the Lord, to Jerusalem"?* (Jer. 3:17a)

In the New Testament age, we are exhorted to speak and sing the Psalms (Eph. 5:19); therefore, we should also obey them. The psalmists reveal God's attitude toward Jerusalem. We are exhorted, *"Pray for the peace of Jerusalem: may they prosper who love you"* (Psa. 122:6). Also, *"If I forget you, O Jerusalem, let my right hand forget its skill! If I do not remember you, let my tongue cling to the roof of my mouth — if I do not exalt Jerusalem above my chief joy"* (Psa. 137:5-6, NKJV).

Many spiritualize these Scriptures totally and apply them to a Gentile Church. They point out that the Church is heavenly Jerusalem… the only Jerusalem important to God. May we never forget that God spoke to Isaiah that the natural city of Jerusalem had become a spiritual harlot, and He therefore called her "Sodom." But He has promised that **this very same city** will have her glory restored as in the beginning! (Isa. 1:8-10, 25-27) Sodom is the name given to natural Jerusalem in both Isaiah and Revelation. After the destruction of natural Jerusalem, it will again be inhabited, as Zechariah 12:6b declares, *"… Jerusalem shall be inhabited again in her own place, even in Jerusalem."* This refers to the Jerusalem that is in Jerusalem, *not* the Jerusalem that is in heaven.

According to Revelation 11:8, Sodom is the name of the city where our Lord was crucified, where His blood was poured out for His people. He will never forget the city for which He wept (Lk. 19:41), for which He cried, *"Jerusalem! Jerusalem!"* (Lk. 13:34), and for which He was crucified! There can be no doubt which Jerusalem the Lord was speaking about in Isaiah — the natural city of Jerusalem that Isaiah knew so well. That natural city will be restored and will continue to be a revelation in the natural realm of the *spiritual* city of Jerusalem, the Bride of Christ. During the Lord's Kingdom, the natural and spiritual (that is, the earthly and the heavenly) will be united. This will also be the case with our natural man and spiritual man. This permanent union will occur during the resurrection and rapture.

Understanding God's plans for Jerusalem explains why such a small city is at the center of world news almost daily, and why one third of the news correspondents of the world are assigned to Jerusalem. Since God calls it *His* city and lays claim to it, Satan, the "god of this world," also has great interest in it. What humility on God's part to lay claim to a city so small and seemingly so insignificant as Jerusalem. Soon, the Lord will place *His* dwelling place there (Jer. 3:17). The battle for Jerusalem rages today, and the Lord declares, *"... in that day will I make Jerusalem a burdensome stone for all people: all that burden themselves with it shall be cut in pieces, though all the people of the earth be gathered together against it"* (Zech. 12:3).

Satan has always wanted to establish his throne in the place where God has chosen to establish His (Isa. 14:13). As the coming of Christ draws near, Satan will seek to control Jerusalem once again through the Gentiles, manifesting himself through wicked men. How assuring to know that the Gentile rule over Jerusalem in the last days will last only 42 months, and afterward, the Lord will return to establish *His* rule over the city and over the world forever! (Rev. 11:2; Dan. 7:25)

Is it not an abomination for Israel to be forced to surrender God's holy hill to the Gentiles after the blood of the nation's youth was shed to win it back in battle? Is it not an even greater abomination for Jerusalem to be given to one of the most vile and deceiving Gentile organizations this world has ever known — the PLO? Is it not an abomination to exalt an international criminal, Yasser Arafat, and allow him to rule over the temple mount, as he does today?

Why did Deputy Defense Minister Mordechai Gur, the colonel whose troops actually took the Old City in 1967, commit suicide on July 16, 1995? The excuse given is that he had cancer and did not want to be a burden to his family. Could the news of Israel's willingness to negotiate over the future of Jerusalem have been a factor in his suicide? After all, he had been a national hero for almost 30 years for taking the holy city, a city that now seemed to be worthless to Israel's government. Was he to interpret this to mean that he had been a hero for a worthless cause?

There were few, if any, in Israel who loved Jerusalem and appreciated its significance to the Jewish faith more than Colonel Gur did in 1967. In his own words, conquering Jerusalem was the "ultimate mission." Jordan controlled the Old City at the time, but during the 1967 war it looked like Jordan might not get involved in the conflict. On July 21, 1995, *The Jerusalem Post* published an article about Colonel Gur explaining that once the 1967 war broke out, the colonel "hoped that Jordan would offer Israel an opportunity to recoup history's 2,000-year-old debt."

The Israeli high command had indicated that they were not interested in capturing Jerusalem. Colonel Gur considered taking the city on his own, using the excuse that he was in hot pursuit of enemy soldiers. He asked himself what "history would say about him as the commander who failed to seize this historic opportunity."

On June 7, 1967, Col. Gur's men accomplished the task they had been given — to take the Mount of Olives on the east side of the Old City. From the mount, he stood viewing the Old City. The *Post* article tells us, "As he surveyed the scene, gripped with emotion, his intelligence officer responded to a call on the radio. It was Central Command relaying an order from Chief of General Staff Yitzhak Rabin. The intelligence officer repeated it aloud to Gur: 'You are to enter the Old City immediately and capture it.' Gur had been waiting for that order for the past 24 hours. More to the point, he felt, the Jewish nation had been waiting for it for 19 centuries."

Col. Gur started down the Mount of Olives immediately, but then felt he should turn around and ascend the mount again. He explained to his staff, "I want to give the command for the conquest of the Old City from an appropriate place." Col. Gur probably did not know just how prophetic his actions were. Very soon, from that very mount, the Lord Jesus Christ, the Captain of the Armies of Heaven, will give the command to conquer the Old City one last time for all eternity! He will descend upon that very mount and fight for Jerusalem (Zech. 14:1-5).

The soldiers who will be with the Lord will be the saints of all ages. Will you be there? Col. Gur may not have fully understood the prophetic import of that moment, but he *did* understand that something deep within the Jewish soul longed to live forever in that city. It is

inconceivable that Israel's negotiations to give that city back to her enemies did not influence Col. Gur to despair of life itself.

The so-called international "Quartet" (The United States, Russia,
the European Union, and the United Nations) began pressuring the Israeli government in December 2002 to give Jerusalem to the Palestinians. If delivering Jerusalem into the hands of Yasser Arafat is, in fact,
an abomination, a logical question would be, What will be the consequences for Israel, and what will be the consequences for the nations
who participate in this travesty?

For some weeks after hearing about the involvement of the United
States in this "Quartet," I felt that this would bring another judgment on
the American people. Some who have been following the unfolding
saga of Israel in the Middle East have been aware of the many times
that God has shouted His displeasure to the United States for pressuring Israel to yield to its enemies. He has spoken through a series of
tragic and devastating events that have occurred in the home states
of at least three sitting presidents. Each time, at the precise moment
that the president was pressuring Israel, a terrible judgment fell on his
own state.

On October 30, 1991, President George Bush opened the Madrid
Conference that would later give rise to the Oslo peace accords, giving
Yasser Arafat sovereignty over key parts of the Holy Land. On that
very day, an extremely unusual storm formed off the coast of Nova
Scotia; it would later be called "The Perfect Storm." It was so impressive that both a book and a movie were made about it. It contained re-
cord-setting 100-foot waves that pounded the New England Coast,
even causing heavy damage to President Bush's home in Kennebunk-
port, Maine. Meteorologists tell us that a "perfect storm" forms only
once every 100 years, but this was not the normal "perfect storm." It
was either a freak accident or a message from God, because it traveled
west for 1,000 miles to reach the United States. Weather patterns in the
United States are almost always west to east, not east to west.

In March 1997, President Clinton received Yasser Arafat at the
White House. Clinton's response at that time was to rebuke Israel for
not keeping its promises to Arafat. He said nothing of the fact that
Arafat had not kept even one of the small promises he had made to Israel. In fact, Arafat had been carefully doing just the opposite of what
he had promised for almost four years. At that very time some of the
worst storms in history broke out, causing record flooding in the Ohio
River. Clinton's home state of Arkansas bore the brunt of those storms.

A *New York Times* front-page article on March 4, 1997, read, "President Clinton Rebukes Israel." The headline of the adjacent article read, "In Storms' Wake: Grief And Shock." The report of Clinton's rebuke was right next to the report of how Clinton's home state had been devastated by some of the worst tornadoes and floods in history, with 13 counties in Arkansas having been declared disaster areas.

On June 8, 2001, George Tenet, the director of the CIA, began talks with senior Israeli and Palestinian officials in Ramallah to pressure Israel into making further concessions to the Palestinians. President George W. Bush had sent him there. The tropical storm Allison had already gone out to sea and had almost ceased to exist. Up until then, that storm had basically been a non-event. At the very hour that Tenet was beginning his meeting, something almost unheard of happened: Allison suddenly revived and changed directions. When it arrived back over Houston, it carried one of the greatest rainfalls in the history of the US. In a period of 24 hours, it dumped almost two and a half feet of water on Houston. An estimated 20,000 homes were destroyed and 50,000 vehicles were lost. Twenty-eight counties in Texas were declared disaster areas by President Bush, who was at home at the time in Crawford, Texas.

February 1, 2003 was another sad and tragic day for Texas and the entire US. The space shuttle suddenly blew up while over Texas as it was preparing to land in Florida. On board was the first Israeli astronaut, Colonel Ilan Ramon. There are hundreds of cities, towns and villages between Texas and Florida, but it blew up over Palestine, Texas. Tragically, the Israeli on board was destined to die over Palestine, and six Americans were destined to die with him. Many more Israelis will die if the US pressures Israel into giving up God's land to a people who have no right to it. They will die "over" Palestine (that is to say, because of Palestine). But so, too, will many more Americans die with them "over" Palestine, because God's protection will not be upon the US in this critical time if we force Israel to yield to her enemies.

How much does God's people and God's land mean to you? Colonel Gur probably committed suicide, at least in part, because of his love for Jerusalem. His reaction was not the correct way to respond to Israel's sorrows. It was a drastic measure. But how will we respond? A drastic measure is definitely in order. In Joel 2:16-17, God exhorts us:

16 Gather the people, sanctify the congregation, assemble the elders, gather the children, and those that suck the breasts: let the bridegroom go forth of his chamber, and the bride out of her closet.

17 Let the priests, the ministers of the LORD, weep between the porch and the altar, and let them say, Spare thy people, O LORD, and give not thine heritage to reproach, that the heathen should rule over them: wherefore should they say among the people, Where is their God?

In life, there are few things more important or sacred to us than our wedding day. To cancel or postpone a wedding, as He exhorts the bride and bridegroom to do in verse 16, demonstrates that a once-in-a-lifetime urgency is confronting them. Doing so is a drastic measure. Nothing else in life is as important or as sacred to the Lord as the future of His people and His land. Is this true for us also? Have His priorities become our priorities? If so, we will respond to His call to intercede that mercy might be extended to Israel. Ezekiel 9:4-6 tells us that a day will come when only those who are sighing and crying for the condition of God's people will be spared. May we all be among that company! Israel's judgment is something that will ultimately touch the life of every person on earth, for better or for worse. Judgment will come on every nation that has participated in dividing God's land (Joel 3:2). But after Israel's judgment, when He has come, He will also bring blessings on all those who have blessed Israel.

Chapter 15

May We Not End Like the General

The news traveled like lightning in the military outpost: in a few minutes, the king would arrive to review the troops. Nervousness gripped the soldiers. Every one, from the highest-ranking officers to the lowliest foot soldiers prepared for the welcome. In a short time, an impeccable military formation awaited the arrival of the king.

The next few minutes seemed like hours. No one could even guess the reason for the delay. But it didn't matter. Everyone in the formation remained at attention. However, one of the generals decided that he could wait quite comfortably while seated, especially since the king's failure to arrive could go on indefinitely. Suddenly, after sleep overcame him, His Royal Highness came bursting into the camp. The general managed to rise from his sleep just as the king approached him.

The king drew near and began rebuking him firmly: "I observed that everyone except you remained at attention, waiting for me, knowing that in spite of my delay I would finally come. But how did you react? You did not sit down because you were tired, but rather, because you doubted my word. Now, not only will I not receive honor from you, but you will remain outside my army forever, because you are not worthy to be a representative of the Crown."

I did not write this story to illustrate the message of this book. In fact, it was written over 120 years ago by a Jewish rabbi named Israel Meir Kegan, also known as Jafetz Jaim. Being an orthodox Jewish rabbi, it is doubtful that he ever read the New Testament or that he was acquainted with the Lord's parable of the ten sleeping virgins. A question that we should all ask ourselves is, "Will the sudden coming of the

King be my wake-up call, or will I receive grace to awaken out of sleep beforehand to faithfully watch and wait for His appearing?

In the Garden of Gethsemane, the Lord's heart was broken because His disciples did not stay awake and weep with the One who was weeping. We find them slumbering and sleeping at a time when they should have been crying out in intercession to the Father, along with the Son. What a tragic picture of the weakness of the flesh. As the Lord sought strength to face the greatest spiritual battle of all time, His disciples slept. Maybe they slept from disappointment and discouragement, as Elijah seemed to do in I Kings 19:4-6, but under the circumstances no reason was justified.

Just before the Cross, the Lord commanded His disciples to pray. Now, just before the Wedding, He has commanded us to rejoice (Rev. 19:7). Those who are sleeping are not obeying His command. To rejoice, even during a delay, is evidence that real faith and trust are in our hearts. May we not be ashamed when the Bridegroom comes... ashamed that we were cast down and discouraged as though the Wedding had been canceled, rather than merely delayed.

Imagine the scene revealed in Revelation 19:1-9 where great joy fills heaven because the Marriage of the Lamb is at hand. Surely, all of heaven is joyfully making the last minute preparations for the most glorious Wedding of all time. Very soon, the great saints and elders of all ages will be gathered around the table of the Marriage Supper of the Lamb. Heaven has awaited this day for thousands of years, and now it is at hand. Nothing could possibly diminish the joy that everyone feels. Nothing, that is, except for one thing. As the saints and angels look toward the earth, they see something tragic—the Lord's Bride is slumbering and sleeping! She is not participating in the joyous celebration and preparations. Some members of the Bride are even losing their vision. Their lamps are going out.

Most weddings are delayed for one reason or another. How would a bridegroom respond if he saw that his lover had fallen asleep during the delay of their wedding? Such a scene would bring indescribable sorrow to his heart. The bridegroom would rightfully respond, "Her heart must not be filled with the same joy that I feel. If she were as happy to marry me as I am to marry her, there is no way that she could fall asleep at such a time."

In our day, the Lord's heart may well be broken again, as it was in Gethsemane, because His disciples are yielding to sleep once more. In

Gethsemane, His disciples did not remain awake to weep with the One who wept, and now His disciples are not remaining awake to rejoice with the One who rejoices. We are commanded to *"Rejoice with those who rejoice, and weep with those who weep"*(Rom. 12:15, NKJV).

Throughout the Bible and history, God's people have almost always failed Him. Will we be any different in the end? The Lord surely has some today who will be like Joshua and Caleb, a delight to His heart among the millions of His people. May we find grace to delight Him in this last hour, rejoicing that the Wedding day is at hand instead of sleeping from disappointment and sorrow that there has been a delay!

Unfortunately, all of the ten virgins slumbered and slept as a result of the bridegroom's delay. Regardless of why they did so during the delay, it could hardly be the right reaction for any of them. Is it any less tragic than when the disciples slept in Gethsemane? They slept, leaving their Savior alone to face, with great sorrow, an overwhelming battle for their own souls. He sorrowed alone (Mark 14:34-37). Today, the ten virgins, who symbolize the Lord's Kingdom, now sleep as their Bridegroom rejoices that the hour for which He died is now at hand—His Marriage. But He rejoices alone, for His Bride slumbers and sleeps.

Some may respond, "But I am not sleeping. I have not departed from the Lord." A person who has entered spiritual slumbering and sleeping has not necessarily departed from the Lord. In Mark 13:32-37 we discover that being asleep in the context of the Lord's coming refers to a person who is no longer watching or looking up in his or her heart. When we sleep, our eyes are closed. We no longer see. Sleeping refers to a lack of vision and expectancy. Also, when we sleep there is a lack of all emotion or expression. We generally are not rejoicing when we are asleep, at least not consciously.

Something else occurs when we are asleep—we dream. Science has discovered that everyone has many dreams during sleep, even those who believe they do not. We simply do not remember most of our dreams, and most are definitely not worth remembering because they are empty, useless and vain thoughts. This type of thoughts fill our spiritual lives when we enter spiritual sleep. Our thoughts are directed to vain and empty things instead of toward that which really matters in life—the Lord and our relationship with Him.

How easy it is for us to set our affection on things on the earth instead of setting it on the Lord! How easy it is to seek earthly things rather than heavenly things! (See Colossians 3:1-2.) This present world is vain, and it is vanity to make earthly goals our pursuit. The Prophet Jonah declared, *"Those who cling to worthless idols forfeit the grace that could be theirs"* (Jon. 2:8, NIV). When the things of this world take first place in our lives, or even when they crowd out our relationship with the Lord, we are asleep spiritually.

As we approach history's greatest moment, it may be that we have yielded to spiritual sleep because of our disappointment from a delay. But, it is time to awake and seek Him; it is not time to sleep. Not only should we seek His presence, but we should also seek to see as He sees and rejoice as He rejoices. The Wedding is at hand! It is time to cast off every distraction and refuse to allow the things and pleasures of this world to consume our time, even though many of those things are legitimate.

I am not encouraging anyone to become a phony super-spiritual person. When this occurs in the lives of parents, for example, they have no time to spend with their children, and they sometimes will not permit their children to develop in any area outside their spiritual lives. This is not pleasing to the Lord and is not true spirituality. I am talking about maintaining a balance in our lives. On the other hand, what many consider to be a "balanced life" is a life with little or no time for spiritual things; their days are filled with the vanities of this world—the dreams and vanities of spiritual sleep. It is time to find a balance where the Lord is at the center of our lives and not merely an additive to help things go better for us.

Although coming under a spiritual sleep, brought on by disappointment, is never God's best for anyone, certainly the five foolish virgins could ill-afford to sleep away the precious time they had been allotted by the Lord's delay. It was time to be paying the price for more oil, not a time for sleeping. Regardless of how much of the oil of His presence we might have, it is time for even the wise virgins to also awake from sleep, to lift up their heads, and to seek the Lord as never before.

Though we have only a minimal understanding of the Lord's prophetic message, we should still be able to recognize that we are living in the time of the end. Will we be sleeping the sleep of discouragement and disappointment when the Lord actually comes for His Bride with a shout of joy? If so, His coming might be an embarrassment to us rather than the joy it should be. We might find ourselves in the position of the general in the rabbi's parable.

It is absolutely amazing that apparently not one person in all of Israel who was alive during the Lord's ministry foresaw the key detail associated with His first coming—that He would die for humanity. Not even His closest disciples could fathom this. It was so hidden from them that even after the Lord told them plainly that He would die and rise again, they were still incapable of grasping this truth. Mark 9:31-32 tells us:

31 For he taught his disciples, and said unto them, The Son of man is delivered into the hands of men, and they shall kill him; and after that he is killed, he shall rise the third day.

32 But they understood not that saying, and were afraid to ask him.

Few of us foresaw the possibility of a delay in the coming of the Bridegroom. Unfortunately, a delay is only one issue that we have failed to see. Surely there are far more transcendental issues regarding the second coming that are still hidden from our eyes. We definitely see through a glass darkly, but we can react to our lack of clear vision in several ways. One possible reaction is that we can decide that, from now on, we will avoid receiving or sharing a vision regarding His coming. This reaction might come from disappointment, or it might be because we do not want to risk the humiliation of being wrong again. Regardless of a person's motivation for avoiding the subject of the last days, doing so produces a tragic result—our spiritual eyes end up being closed in sleep.

Besides the timing of the Lord's coming, there are surely many other important details regarding His coming that He wants to show us. We might need to know some of them for our own spiritual well being in these last days. However, they will all remain hidden from the sleeping soul. Let us not be content to slumber and sleep any longer. Whether you feel that the message of this book is right or not, I trust that each of us will hear and obey the call to arise from our sleep and seek the Lord. It is time to seek Him for new and greater understanding of our times and His coming. It is time to rejoice with all our hearts with the Bridegroom because the Wedding is at hand!

For more information write to any of the following addresses:

Hebron Ministries
P.O. Box 4274
Leesburg, VA   20177-8388 U.S.A.

Hebron Ministries (Worldwide)
Section 0374 P.O. Box 02-5289
Miami, Florida   33102-5289 U.S.A.

minheb@c.net.gt

Or call:
1-800-LAST-DAY
(1-800-527-8329)
in the United States

or
(502) 333-2615
in Guatemala, Central America

Other Books Available...

The Final Victory: The Year 2000?
By Marvin Byers

Discover why this book is a bestseller. It reveals what the early Church and also the Jewish people believed regarding God's timetable for the coming of Christ. The Great Tribulation and the Rapture are also examined in light of unmistakable biblical declarations that contradict many popular private interpretations. The year 2000 has passed, but it is still critically urgent for God's people to have an unshakeable understanding of the end. This book explains why, as never before, a clear understanding of the end is a life-and-death issue and not merely an unnecessary spiritual luxury.

TPB-396 p.   ISBN 1-56043-824-X   Retail $12.99

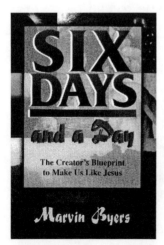

Six Days and a Day
The Creator's Blueprint
to Make Us Like Jesus
By Marvin Byers

Do you long to be like Jesus? You can be, if you follow God's blueprint for your life. The Creation account in Genesis, like every other miracle of Christ in the Bible ,is full of truth and reveals God's ways and nature. Only the Creator could make a glorious new creation out of absolutely nothing. He wants to do the same in your life, making you into a new creation in Christ that is filled with the glory of the last Adam—the Lord Himself!

TPB-240 p. ISBN 1-56043-263-2 Retail $12.99

Yasser Arafat
An Apocalyptic Character?
The Middle East—What is Happening and How it Will Affect You
By Marvin Byers

Daniel gives approximately 80 prophetic details to help us identify the little horn when he comes. Yasser Arafat has fulfilled almost 50 of these and is poised to fulfill the others very soon. Could Yasser Arafat be part of the fulfillment of God's prophetic message? Also, could it be that the prophetic message is being fulfilled before our eyes, and we do not see nor hear what is happpening? Consider the facts presented in this incredible book and decide for yourself. Available in audio cassette.

TPB-262 p.   ISBN 0-9647871-3-X   Retail $12.99

The Mystery: A Lost Key
Israel and the Gentile Church:
A life and death issue for all believers

By Marvin Byers

The relationship between Israel and the Gentile Church is called a "mystery" by the Apostle Paul. He shows that this issue is the most important truth after the gospel of salvation. Sadly, it is almost totally ignored in the Church today. According to Paul, the mystery:
- Is the source of abundant grace
- Will keep us from falling in the time of shaking
- Is the key to real authority and real victory in spiritual warfare
- Is the key to experiencing the fullness of Christ's life flowing in us
- Will allow us to be part of the kingdom of God and inherit the earth

Paul shows that the right faith regarding the mystery determines if we receive the above blessings.

TPB-160 p.   ISBN 0-9647871-9-9   Retail $8.99